WHEN THE STARS REMEMBERED ME

For The Ones Who Chose Silence as Their Voice

Anvita Jain

BlueRose ONE.com DIY
Stories Matter
NewDelhi • London

BLUEROSE PUBLISHERS
India | U.K.

For permissions requests or inquiries regarding this publication,
please contact:

BLUEROSE PUBLISHERS
www.BlueRoseONE.com
info@bluerosepublishers.com
+91 8882 898 898
+4407342408967

ISBN: 978-93-7542-108-5

First Edition: February 2026

We don't always get the apologies we deserve.
But maybe.... healing isn't about
hearing "I'm sorry." It's about learning
to say,
"I'm free."
Free from expectations. Free from the fear of being
left out.
Free from the desire to be acknowledged.

PROLOGUE

Forgotten Light

Airi Takahashi learned very early that silence could be louder than any sound.

In her house, voices were never raised in anger. There was no shouting, no slammed doors, no obvious cruelty. Instead, there was laughter—warm, bright laughter that floated through the rooms like sunlight but it just never seemed to reach her.

She grew up watching it from the edges.

Their attention moved instinctively toward her younger sister, Mio—toward her energy, her questions, her excitement. Mio's presence filled space effortlessly, like music playing without being asked to. Her parents' smiles always arrived before she entered a room and faded just as quickly after she left.

Airi learned to make herself smaller.

She learned how to walk quietly across the floor so no one would sigh at the sound of her footsteps. She learned to answer questions briefly, to smile politely, to never interrupt. She learned that wanting too much—wanting to be noticed, wanting to be held, wanting to be chosen, wanting to be loved, wanting to be seen—only made the ache worse.

So, she stopped asking and ironically no one noticed her changing slowly, no one noticed her dying slowly in her own house. Dying in ways she can't explain and in ways she prayed no one should ever. In ways that you feel like something inside you is breaking but you don't know what so eventually you can't explain that feeling to anyone and the worst case is when that happens to you because of you own family.

Her room became her refuge. Not because it was lonely, but because it was honest. The walls were lined with sketchbooks stacked carefully, their pages heavy with charcoal shadows and star-filled skies. Her desk was always neat, paintbrushes cleaned and aligned, as if order could make up for everything else that felt scattered inside her. As if cleaning form outside would help her keep peace with her inner scattered self.

Art was the only place where she allowed herself to exist fully.

When she was thirteen, she realized something strange: it hurt less to pour everything onto paper than to wait for someone to ask how she was doing. Her drawings began to change then. Faces turned away from the viewer. Hands reached upward. Skies grew wider, deeper, more endless than before.

The stars appeared again and again.

At seventeen, when she won a national art competition, she thought—just for a moment—that things might finally change.

She stood in the living room holding the envelope, her fingers trembling not from excitement but from hope. Her parents were busy, voices overlapping as they discussed decorations and guest lists. Mio's birthday was coming up. It was all everyone seemed to talk about.

"Mom," Airi said softly. "Dad."

They looked at her, distracted but present enough to hear the words. "I won," she said. "My painting... it was selected."

There was a pause. Her mother smiled vaguely, as though trying to place the importance of what she'd just heard.

"That's nice, Airi," she said. "Could you help me later? We still need to finish the balloons."

That was all.

That night, Airi stood by her bedroom window, the city quiet beneath her, the sky stretched wide above her head. Stars scattered across the darkness, distant and cold and impossibly steady.

"If I disappeared," she whispered into the night, her breath fogging the glass, "Would anyone finally look for me?"

The stars didn't answer.

But they didn't turn away either.

That night she finally learnt that keeping hopes from the people who don't even bother is the worst thing she could do to herself. So, since that day she stopped expecting and the things started changing.

"If I disappear, maybe they'll finally look at me."

CHAPTER ONE

The Unseen Morning

Morning arrived gently in Airi's room.

Soft sunlight slipped through the thin curtains, brushing against the corner of her desk, catching on the edges of unfinished sketches. Dust particles floated in the air, slow and weightless, as if even time itself moved more carefully here.

Airi sat on the edge of her bed, tying her hair in front of the mirror.

The mirror was old, a faint crack running diagonally across its surface. It split her reflection in two—one side clear, the other slightly distorted. She had stared at that crack so often that she barely noticed it anymore. Still, sometimes she wondered if it reflected something truer than the unbroken glass ever could.

Her face looked calm. It always did.

But her eyes were tired in a way sleep never seemed to fix.

"In this house," she thought, looping her hair into a low ponytail, "silence feels louder than words."

From downstairs, her mother's voice drifted upward, bright

and urgent. “Mio! Breakfast is ready! Hurry, or you’ll be late!”

Airi paused for just a second, her fingers tightening around the hair tie. No one called her name.

She finished tying her hair, stood up, and smoothed the wrinkles from her uniform. The movement was automatic, practiced. She had learned long ago how to prepare herself without being prompted.

“I’m already here,” she murmured, the words barely audible even to herself.

The sound of plates clinking echoed from the kitchen. Chairs scraped softly against the floor. Life continued, full and complete, without waiting for her.

At the breakfast table, the air was warm and familiar. Mio sat across from her, eyes bright, swinging her legs slightly as she talked. Their parents listened closely, nodding, smiling, asking questions that showed genuine interest.

“Mio, your presentation was wonderful,” her mother said, placing another dish in front of her. “Your teacher called me personally.”

Mio grinned. “Really? I was nervous, but I’m glad it went well!”

“That’s my girl,” her father added proudly. “Keep this up, and you’ll get into one of the best schools in Tokyo.”

Airi lowered her gaze to her bowl of rice and ate quietly. Each bite tasted the same—warm, bland, unremarkable.

Mio glanced at her, tilting her head. “Onee-chan, you’re eating so slowly again."

Airi forced a small smile. "I just woke up late." There was a brief silence.

No one responded.

Her parents continued talking as if the moment had never existed, as if her voice had dissolved into the air before it could reach them.

"Even when I speak," Airi thought, her chest tightening just slightly, "it's like my voice gets lost somewhere between my heart and the room."

She finished breakfast, stood, and quietly carried her bowl to the sink. No one stopped her. No one noticed when she left.

At school, hallways buzzed with energy. Laughter bounced off the walls. Shoes hurried across polished floors. Names were called, greetings exchanged, moments shared.

Mio walked ahead of her, surrounded by friends. Airi followed a few steps behind, holding her sketch folder close to her chest.

A group of classmates passed them.

"Your sister's amazing at art, right?" one of them said to Mio. Mio laughed lightly. "Ah... yeah. She's okay, I guess."

The words weren't cruel.

And yet, they landed quietly, heavily, somewhere deep inside Airi. The words weren't meant to hurt but they did break something inside her.

She didn't stop walking.

In art class, Ms. Nakamura paused at her desk, lifting one of her sketches carefully. It showed a girl sitting alone beneath a tree, shadows stretching long across the ground.

"This is beautiful," the teacher said softly. "The emotion... it's rare. Where did you learn to draw like this?"
Airi hesitated. "I just... draw what I feel."

Ms. Nakamura smiled. "You should enter the National Art Competition. Sometimes the quietest hearts create the loudest art."

For a moment, something warm stirred inside Airi's chest.

On the rooftop later that day, wind tugged gently at her hair as she sketched beneath the open sky. She didn't notice Ren Kurosawa until his shadow fell across her page.

"You're always up here alone," he said, not accusing—just

observing. She looked up, startled. "I like the view."

He glanced at her sketch. "You draw feelings. Not

just shapes." Her fingers tightened around her

pencil.
"Feelings," she said quietly, "are all I have."

Ren looked at her then—not past her, not

through her. Just at her.

And for the first time that day, Airi felt something unfamiliar settle gently in her chest.

The feeling of being seen.

I thought art could fill the cracks in my heart. But maybe.... Some cracks were never meant to close; we are just meant to live with them forever.

CHAPTER TWO

Silence at the Table

Dinner was supposed to be the time when families came together.

That was what Airi had read in books, what teachers spoke about with fond smiles, what television dramas showed so easily—parents asking about school, siblings arguing softly, laughter filling the space between shared dishes.

In the Takahashi house, dinner happened every night at precisely seven.

The clock above the kitchen ticked steadily as plates were placed on the table. Steam rose gently from bowls of soup, carrying familiar smells that should have felt comforting. Airi took her seat quietly, folding her hands in her lap, waiting.

Mio burst into the room seconds later, energy spilling ahead of her.

"Mom! Dad! You won't believe it—my friend Aya says the class trip might be to Kyoto!"

Her parents reacted instantly.

"Kyoto?" her mother repeated with delight. "That's

wonderful!" "You'll love it," her father added. "We should

start planning already."

Airi listened, her gaze drifting to the surface of the table. The wood had tiny scratches, worn smooth over time. She traced one of them lightly with her finger, grounding herself.

The conversation flowed easily—school gossip, upcoming events, future plans that sparkled with excitement. Mio's laughter rang bright and clear, filling every corner of the room.

Airi waited.

She always

did.

She waited for the pause where someone might turn to her and ask, "how was your day?"
She waited for her name to be spoken with intention instead of obligation.

It never came.

Halfway through the meal, her mother sighed. "Mio, don't forget—you have piano practice tomorrow."
"I know," Mio said cheerfully. "I'm already better than

last week." Her father chuckled. "Of course, you are."

Airi swallowed slowly. Her spoon felt heavier than usual.

"I had art club today," she said softly, the words slipping out before she could stop them.

Three pairs of eyes flickered toward her—briefly.

"That's nice," her mother said automatically, already reaching for another topic. "Mio, did you finish your homework?"

"Yes!"

The attention shifted again, quick and effortless.

Airi felt something inside her chest tighten—not sharply, but steadily, like a knot pulled just a little tighter every day.
She lowered her head and continued eating.

Maybe, she thought, if I speak less, it won't hurt as much.

After dinner, she cleared her plate and moved toward the sink. The sound of running water filled the room as she washed dishes methodically, her movements precise and controlled.

Behind her, her parents and sister talked about weekend plans. There was mention of shopping, a movie, maybe ice cream afterward.

No one asked if she wanted to come.

When she finished, she dried her hands carefully and slipped upstairs unnoticed.
In her room, the door closed with a soft click.

Airi leaned against it for a moment, eyes closed,

breathing slowly. "I don't hate them," she told herself.

"They're just... not looking."

She moved to her desk and opened a sketchbook. The blank page stared back at her, wide and empty.

She picked up a pencil.

Her hand moved almost on its own, lines forming without conscious thought. A girl sat at a table, surrounded by people whose faces were blurred, their attention turned elsewhere.

Shadows stretched across the floor, long and heavy.

Airi stared at the drawing when she

finished. "This is how it feels," she

whispered.

And for once, the silence answered back.
No matter what I do.... It's never enough.
I thought they'd be proud....
But it's just another sound lost in their laughter.

CHAPTER THREE

Hallways Full of Voices

School hallways were never quiet.

They pulsed with sound—footsteps, laughter, lockers slamming shut, voices overlapping in bursts of excitement and complaint. To most people, it was chaos. To Airi, it was proof that the world moved loudly and confidently without her.

She walked through it like a ghost.

Mio's friends greeted her enthusiastically, arms looping around her shoulders as they talked all at once. Airi followed a short distance behind, her steps measured, her presence barely registered.

She didn't blame them.

People saw what stood in front of them. And Airi had learned how to fade into the background too well.

In class, teachers praised Mio's participation, calling her name often, encouraging her curiosity. Airi answered when spoken to, her responses precise and thoughtful, but rarely extended beyond what was required.

“Good answer, Takahashi,” a teacher said once, already turning back to the board.

Not Mio Takahashi.

Just Takahashi.

During lunch, Airi sat near the window, sketchbook open, pencil moving softly across the page. She preferred this—observing rather than engaging. The world made more sense when translated into lines and shadows.

Across the room, she noticed Ren Kurosawa sitting alone, staring at his phone without really looking at it. He was quiet too, but in a different way. His silence felt chosen, not forced.

She glanced away quickly when she realized she was staring.

Later, on the rooftop, the sky stretched endlessly above her. Clouds drifted lazily, unconcerned with anything below them. Airi sketched there often. The open space made it easier to breathe for her. She was halfway through a drawing when footsteps approached.

“You’re here again.”

She looked up, startled, to see Ren standing a few steps away, hands in his pockets, eyes curious rather than intrusive. “I like it here,” she said cautiously. He nodded. “It’s quieter.” The wind moved between them, gentle but persistent.

He leaned closer, peering at her sketch. “You draw like you’re trying to say something.”

Airi hesitated.

"Sometimes," she said, "it's easier to draw than to talk." She continued, "when people can't explain what they feel they choose to draw, write, or even sing because that helps them to explain it well."

Ren straightened, studying her face. "Does it help?"

She considered the question carefully. "It stops things from overflowing. It stops us from getting out of our own sanity."

He didn't ask what she meant.

"I think," he said slowly, "that's why it feels so real."

Airi's chest warmed at the word.
Real.
No one had ever described her work like that before.

As the bell rang below them, echoing faintly through the building, Airi packed up her things.

Ren lingered for a moment.
"If you don't mind," he said, "I'd like to see more of your drawings sometime." She nodded, unsure why her heart felt suddenly lighter.

As he walked away, Airi looked up at the sky once more. The clouds were shifting, slowly revealing patches of blue.
For the first time that day, she didn't feel completely invisible.

When the world stops looking for you....
you start wondering if you were never really meant to be there.

CHAPTER FOUR

The Rooftop Where Wind Spoke

The rooftop became a quiet promise.

Not spoken aloud, not acknowledged directly—but understood.

After that day, Airi found herself arriving there earlier, her steps lighter, her anticipation carefully hidden even from herself. The sky greeted her the same way each time—vast, patient, endlessly open. But something within her had shifted, just slightly.

She wasn't alone anymore.

Ren appeared a few minutes after her, as he often did. Sometimes he brought nothing but himself. Other times, a book he didn't read or a phone he barely checked. He never crowded her space. He never asked questions she wasn't ready to answer.

They sat near each other, separated by silence that didn't feel heavy.

"Your lines changed," Ren said one afternoon, nodding toward her sketchbook. Airi glanced down. "Changed how?"

"They're softer," he said. "Like you're not pressing as hard."

She studied the page. He was right. The shadows were still there, but they no longer swallowed the figures whole. Light slipped through more freely now.

"I didn't notice," she admitted.

Ren shrugged. "Maybe you're breathing more."

The wind picked up, tugging at loose pages. Airi held the sketchbook steady, heart beating a little faster than usual.

"Why do you come up here?" she asked, surprising herself.

Ren leaned back against the fence; eyes lifted to the sky. "It's the only place where I don't feel like I have to explain myself. Here I think no one could judge me for who I am or what I am doing."

She understood that instantly.

"My house is loud," he continued. "Not angry. Just... crowded. Expectations everywhere. Up here, no one needs anything from me. It's just me and the sky."

Airi nodded slowly. "In my house," she said, voice barely above the wind, "it's quiet. But not peaceful. Quiet in a way that I wish no one has to face. It haunts sometimes."

Ren turned to look at her.

She almost regretted saying it—but he didn't push. He didn't demand details. He simply listened.

"That sounds lonely," he said.

The word settled gently between them.

"Yes," Airi replied. "It is."

The bell rang again, distant and dull. Neither of them moved right away.

As they packed up, Ren hesitated. “There’s an art exhibition downtown this weekend,” he said casually. “I thought... maybe you’d like it.”

Airi’s first instinct was to decline.

Crowds made her shrink inward. New places felt like tests she hadn’t studied for. New people always made her uneasy and it always felt like she is under the constant pressure of being judged.

She never liked crowded places or opening up to people about anything.

But then she remembered the way he looked at her drawings. The way he listened. To the surprise it gave her the courage to do that this time.

“I’ll think about it,” she said.

He smiled—not wide, not triumphant. Just hopeful.

That night, alone in her room, Airi stared at the ceiling long after the lights were out. Her sketchbook lay open beside her, a half-finished drawing of two figures sitting beneath an open sky.

“They’re not touching,” she thought, tracing the outlines with her eyes. “But they’re not alone either.”

For the first time in a long while, sleep came easily.

For the first time she wasn’t forcing herself to breath, it just happened.

It’s not perfect.... But it’s me.
Broken yet beautiful.

CHAPTER FIVE

Cracks That Never Healed

Some memories never faded.

They waited patiently, resurfacing in quiet moments when Airi least expected them—when the house was too still, when laughter echoed from a room, she wasn't part of, when she caught her reflection and wondered how long she had been holding her breath. When one day, on a sudden evening while you are sitting, the past knocks uninformed. That breaks you in a way not even you could imagine.
She was eight the first time she noticed.
It was her birthday.
Airi sat at the dining table, legs swinging nervously, a small cake placed in front of her. The candles burned steadily, their flames trembling just slightly. She had chosen the cake herself—plain, with strawberries on top.

Her parents were late.

Minutes stretched long. The candles melted down, wax pooling at their bases. When her parents finally arrived, apologetic but distracted, they sang hurriedly and cut the cake unevenly.

Later that evening, she overheard her mother on the phone.

"I forgot the time," she said with a laugh. "It's fine—Airi doesn't really mind these things."
Airi stood in the hallway, holding a plate of uneaten cake.

She learned then that disappointment was easier to swallow quietly then to show to people who don't even care.
At eleven, she won her first local art prize. Her teacher hugged her on stage. Her schoolmates clapped. Something was missing, her parents at that event.
She for the first time felt alone even though she was surrounded with a lot of people who were genuinely happy for her. That day she understood that even the absence of one person can empty your whole world.
She rushed home with the certificate pressed carefully against her chest. Her parents glanced at it briefly.

"That's good," her father said. "But Mio has her recital tonight. We need to leave soon."

The certificate ended up folded inside a drawer.

She wanted to ask them *why weren't they present at the ceremony.* She wanted to ask more questions to her parents but stayed silent.
At fourteen, she stopped mentioning her achievements altogether.
At sixteen, she stopped expecting anything.
Now, at seventeen, sitting alone on her bed, Airi flipped through old sketchbooks. The progression was obvious. The earlier drawings were crowded, heavy with dark strokes. Later ones showed space—distance, longing, unanswered questions.

"You learn to leave room for what never came," she murmured

"but eventually that never came and the room remained vacant which no one bothered to fill."

Her phone buzzed.

A message from Ren.

Are you coming to the exhibition tomorrow?

She stared at the screen for a long

moment. Then she typed:
Yes.

Her heart beat unevenly as she pressed send.

She didn't know it yet, but that single decision—small and quiet—would begin to pull at the cracks she had learned to live with.

And sometimes, cracks were where the light entered.

CHAPTER SIX

The Weight of Being Unwanted

The house felt different when night settled in.

During the day, sunlight softened the corners, and movement filled the spaces between rooms. At night, everything became sharper—shadows stretched longer, and the quiet pressed in from all sides.

Airi sat on the edge of her bed, her sketchbook open but untouched.

Downstairs, laughter drifted upward. Mio's voice rang bright as she talked about something trivial—something happy. Her parents responded warmly, their words overlapping, alive with interest.

Airi listened without meaning to.

She had learned the rhythm of these sounds over the years. The pauses where she might have been invited into the conversation. The moments when her name could have fit naturally between sentences.

It never did. The silence in her world haunted her but she wasn't able to express it except in her arts.

She closed her sketchbook slowly.

"I don't think they hate me," she thought. "That would almost be easier."

Hate required attention. Dislike meant acknowledgment.

Ignorance is the only thing that doesn't demand anything not even that person.

What hurt most was the absence—the way her existence seemed optional, easily overlooked without consequence.

She stood and walked to the window. The city lights below shimmered softly, distant and indifferent. Somewhere among them were families finishing dinner together, siblings arguing over television channels, parents asking questions they genuinely wanted answers to.

Airi pressed her forehead lightly against the

cool glass.

"What am I missing?" she whispered.

The room offered no reply.

Later, her mother knocked briefly before opening the door. "Airi, don't stay up too late. You have school tomorrow."

"Yes," Airi said automatically.

Her mother hesitated, as if searching for something

else to say. Then she left.

The door closed gently, but the silence that followed felt heavier than before.

Airi sat back down on her bed and opened her sketchbook again. This time, her pencil moved quickly, urgently. Lines formed without hesitation—too sharp, too dark.

A figure stood at the edge of a space too wide to cross. On the other side, blurred shapes faced away, unaware.

Art was the only escape for her when the world becomes too cruel to her. She stopped suddenly, her hand trembling.

“I’m tired,” she admitted quietly. “Of being strong in ways no one sees. So tired of living with false expectations that someday my parents would love me but it had never happened...... and now I am just tired.”

The thought lingered, heavier than she expected.

CHAPTER SEVEN

The Bridge of Goodbyes

The next day while Airi was returning home, her school bag slung loosely over her shoulder.

She glanced across the street – saw her parents waiting for Mio at her dance academy.

"They're early again," she thought, "For her."

She runs out, her parents hugging her proudly. Airi stops walking, watching from across the road.

I should be used to it by now. But every time I see it.... It still hurts. It still breaks something inside me whenever I watch them happy without me. I wish I was never born.

She turns away and walks home.

***

At the dinner table, laughter filled the room but Airi's seat remained empty. Her mother noticed her untouched plate.

"Where is Airi? Didn't she come home early?"

"Probably studying," her father said. "You know how she is – always quiet." Mio as always, smilingly said, "She said she is tired lately... maybe she needs some rest."

"She should be more like you, Mio," her mother said. "Always cheerful."

That night Airi sat by her window, drowning in her own thoughts while drawing.

Even in my drawings.... I can't even make myself stand out. I think it would have been better if I'd never been a part of their life. They would have had a great, happy family.

She puts down her pencil, tears in her eyes. A phone notification lights up – a message from Ren.

"Hey, stargazer. You up?

I found a new place where you can see the night sky clearly. Wanna come tomorrow?"

She stared at it, then types slowly.

"Maybe... but if I disappear, you still look at the stars, right?"

That night the town slept. The sky was overcast, Airi walked alone. Streetlights flickered on one by one, casting pale halos onto damp pavement.

The air smelled faintly of rain, the kind that came slowly, almost thoughtfully. She clutched her sketchbook tightly to her chest.

Her footsteps echoed softly as she moved forward, each one measured, deliberate—not rushed, not frantic. Inside her, everything felt strangely calm, as though the storm had already passed and left only stillness behind.

"I don't want to disappear because I'm weak," she told herself. "I just don't know how to keep existing like this."

She never wished to disappear, all she ever wanted was to be found.... but life always has its own plans.

The bridge loomed ahead, quiet and nearly empty. Cars passed occasionally below, their sounds distant, detached from her world.

She leaned against the railing, looking out at the dark water.

Her reflection stared back faintly from the metal—distorted, incomplete.

Airi opened her sketchbook to a blank page. She didn't write a letter to her family.

She didn't list reasons or accusations. Instead, she drew the stars. Small at first. Then many. She wrote beneath them, her handwriting steady but light:

I tried to be quiet.
I tried to be good.
I tried to be invisible.
If I leave, please remember that I existed.

This was not something out of hatred but because sometimes we feel like life hasn't left any options with us.

Her breath hitched, just once.

She closed the book carefully, as if sealing something precious inside. Above her, clouds shifted, revealing a faint scattering of stars.

"They're still there," she thought distantly. "Even when you forget to look, they are always watching you from up there."

Ren stared at the last message of Airi for a long time, searching for the meaning behind these words.

Airi you have been acting strange lately.

He looks at his window – the moonlight reflecting on his phone screen.

His intuitions shouting loudly that something is wrong.

CHAPTER EIGHT

The Night That Wouldn't Let Her Go

Her mind was quiet in a frightening way. Not peaceful—hollow. Like a room where all the furniture had been removed, leaving only echoes.

That was when she

heard it. "Airi!"

The sound didn't register immediately.

Her name felt foreign, like it belonged to

someone else. "Airi—please!"

She turned slowly, her movements delayed, as if her body and mind were no longer working together. Ren stood several steps away, rain already soaking through his clothes, his chest rising and falling unevenly.

He had been running.

"You shouldn't be here," she said, her voice distant even to herself. “It’s dangerous.”

Ren shook his head violently. “You’re the one who shouldn’t be here.” He took a step closer.

“Don’t come any nearer,” she whispered—not as a warning, but as a plea. “I don’t even trust myself to think clearly right now.”

Rain began to fall harder now, blurring the edges of the world. The streetlights smeared into soft halos, trembling with each drop. Ren stopped where he was.

“Then let me think for you,” he said, his voice breaking. “Just for tonight.” Her grip on the sketchbook loosened.

The ground felt unsteady. Her legs trembled, not from fear, but from exhaustion so deep it felt bone-deep. The weight she had carried for years— being unnoticed, unchosen, unheard—pressed down all at once.

“I’m so tired,” she said, the words slipping out before she could stop them. “I tried so hard to be easy to be loved but no one cared. Now all I want is peace.” Ren’s breath caught.

“You never had to earn it,” he said desperately. “You were always enough.” The world tilted.

Airi felt herself slipping—not falling forward, not backward, just... away. Consciousness blurred at the edges, thoughts dissolving into fragments.

She remembered Ren shouting her name again.

Then hands—firm, shaking, holding her shoulders, anchoring her to something solid when everything else felt like it was drifting away.

“Stay with me,” he said over and over, voice hoarse, as if the repetition itself might keep her here. “Just stay. Please”

Rain soaked through her clothes, cold and grounding. The railing pressed against her side. Ren braced himself, refusing to let go even as his arms burned and his balance faltered.

For a moment, Airi felt nothing at all.

Then—pressure.

Warmth.

The sound of someone breathing too fast, too close.

“I’ve got you,” Ren whispered, more to himself than to her. “I won’t let go.”

Darkness closed in—not gently, not violently. Just completely.

CHAPTER NINE

When Eyes Open Again

Airi woke to the sound of machines.

Soft beeping. A steady rhythm that reminded her of time moving forward whether she was ready or not.

Her eyelids felt heavy, as if opening them required permission she wasn't sure she had. When she finally did, light flooded her vision—too bright, too sharp. She blinked slowly.

A hospital room.

For several seconds, she didn't understand why she

was there. Then memory returned in pieces.

Rain.
Her name being shouted.
Hands holding her so tightly it hurt.
Her chest tightened.

"I'm alive,"

She realized.

Not with relief.
With confusion.

Ren was asleep in the chair beside her bed, head tilted forward, fingers still curled around the edge of the mattress as if afraid she might disappear if he let go.

She watched him quietly.

He looked exhausted in a way she had never seen before—like someone who had used every ounce of strength they had and still hadn't felt it was enough.
Guilt settled heavy in her stomach. "I did this," she thought. "To him."
Her parents arrived later that day.
They entered together, standing stiffly at the foot of the bed, their expressions tight with worry—but not the kind that reached all the way to their eyes.

Her mother spoke first. "How are you feeling?"
Airi searched her face for something—something—familiar.
"I don't know," she answered honestly.
Her father nodded absently, already glancing at his phone. "The doctor said you'll recover soon, physically."

Physically.

Her mother sighed, pressing a hand to her forehead. "Mio hasn't been sleeping well since last night. She keeps asking questions."
Airi's chest hollowed out. "I see," she said quietly.
"We didn't know how to explain it to her," her father continued.
"She's very sensitive."
Sensitive.

They talked for several more minutes—about schedules, about school absences, about how shocking everything had been for them.

No one asked what it felt like to wake up unsure if you were allowed to exist. No one asked why she had reached that breaking point.

No one asked how she has been lately.

Eventually, they left.

Airi's questions remained unanswered....
Their footsteps faded down the hallway, unhurried.
Airi stared at the door long after it closed.
"So, this is it," she thought.
"Even now."
Even now it's all about Mio that's going in their heads. What about me?
Why am I still living?

Ren woke shortly after.

He noticed her eyes open and froze, as if afraid the moment wasn't real. "You're awake," he said softly.

She nodded.

He reached into his bag, hesitating before pulling something out.

"I didn't know if this was okay," he said quietly. "But I thought... maybe you'd need it."
He placed a new sketchbook gently into her hands.

The cover was dark blue, speckled faintly like a night sky.

"I saw it at the store near the hospital," he continued. "It reminded me of your drawings."
Airi ran her fingers over the cover.
And placed it in the side table of her bed.

Something in her chest cracked open—not painfully, but deeply. "Thank you," she whispered.

Ren swallowed hard. "You don't have to draw anything yet. Or ever. I just... wanted you to have a place to put things. When you're ready."
She didn't respond.
For the first time since waking up, tears slipped down her cheeks.
Ren didn't say anything.
He stayed.

"Why have you saved me?" she said while the stream of tears falling down her face "You should have let me died."
"Why...."

"Calm down Airi." Ren said "The future ahead of you will be worth living moreover you can't just die like that without showing me the sky of your own galaxy."
"I'll never let you go or face anything alone
Airi. Remember you matter."
"I never said you to save me.... so why.... No one really cares if I die. So let me die.... what's the issue...." Airi said while crying uncontrollably.

Ren reaching towards Airi while trying to console her said, "Airi remember you don't have to ask anyone anything and you are enough. I am always here. For now, just promise me that you'll live, even if it's not what you want but for me.... Please" as he continued to hug her.

CHAPTER TEN

Leaving Without Being Stopped

Recovery wasn't dramatic.
It didn't come with sudden clarity or gratitude.
It came with silence.
It came with a burdened promise.

At home, everything looked the same—the furniture, the walls, the routines. And that sameness hurt more than anything else ever could.

Her parents were careful now. Too careful. They watched her constantly, their concern hovering but shallow, like hands that never quite touched.
Mio avoided her eyes.

Sometimes Airi caught her standing outside her door, hesitating, then walking away.
No one talked about what had happened. It became an unspoken rule.
Airi understood then.

If she stayed, she would fade again—not because anyone wanted her to, but because it was easier that way.

One morning, she packed.
Not angrily.
Not secretly.
Just quietly.
Her mother noticed first. "Are you... going somewhere?"
"Yes," Airi said calmly. "Tokyo."
Her parents exchanged a glance.
"When will you be back?" her father asked.
"I don't know."
There was a pause.

No one told her to stay.

No one followed her to the door.

As she stepped outside, the air felt lighter, unfamiliar, but breathable.

As she was leaving, her tears stream down her cheeks, not out of the sadness of leaving her house but in the little happiness of finally leaving the place that hurt her the most.

You can't heal in the same environment where you got hurt. She read it somewhere and now she has finally understood it.
"Airi" Ren was standing just behind her.

"Airi.... Remember you are stronger than you think you are. I am always with you.
Now that you have taken the decision of a fresh start don't look back, please.... Everything in the future will turn out in you favor and remember the promise that you made me."
"Will you come visit?" Airi asked Ren.

"I promise I will." Ren continued, "And the next time I visit, I want to see your new drawings, not the ones from this. The ones which would be drawn with peace not pain."

On the train, she opened the new sketchbook for the first time that Ren gave her.
The first page remained blank.

And for once, that felt like permission.

CHAPTER ELEVEN

Tokyo Is Loud, But I Can Breathe

Tokyo did not welcome Airi gently.

It arrived all at once—noise layered over noise, people moving in every direction with purpose she didn't yet have. Train doors slid open and shut with mechanical precision. Announcements echoed overhead. Footsteps blended into a constant hum that never truly faded.

For a moment, standing on the platform with her bag at her feet, Airi felt small again.

But this time, it was different. This time she was relaxed.

The noise wasn't pressing in on her. It wasn't demanding anything.

It simply existed and so does she.

She took a breath. It came easily.

***

Her apartment was small—smaller than she had imagined—but it was hers. The walls were bare, the floor cool beneath her feet. Sunlight filtered in through a narrow window, catching dust in the air and turning it briefly into something almost beautiful.

She set her bag down and stood in the center of

the room. "This is enough," she told herself.

The first few days passed quietly. Too quietly, at times. Without school bells or family routines, time stretched in unfamiliar ways. Airi woke early, unsure what she was supposed to do with herself once she was awake.

But the quietness was peaceful in a way she

can't explain. She explored the neighborhood

slowly.

A bakery on the corner that smelled like sugar and warmth. A narrow street lined with vending machines humming softly to themselves. A small park tucked between buildings where elderly couples fed pigeons in comfortable silence and in the evening, children play without worrying about what's coming next or how are they going to survive this cruel world.

Not knowing everything is also a blessing. It allows us to

live freely. No one knew her here.

And strangely, that felt like relief rather

than loss. At night, the city glowed.

From her window, she watched lights flicker on and off across distant buildings, each one belonging to someone else's life. The world felt vast in a way it never had back home.

“I didn’t disappear here,” she thought. “I just haven’t been discovered yet.”

She opened the new sketchbook Ren had given her and placed it on the floor in front of her. For a long time, she didn’t touch it. She simply sat beside it, knees drawn to her chest, listening to the muffled sounds of the city beyond the walls.

Her phone buzzed.

A message from Ren.

Did you arrive safely?

She stared at the screen before replying.

Yes. I’m here.

Three dots appeared almost immediately.

Good. I was worried.

Airi hesitated, then typed:

It’s loud.

Another pause.

Is that okay? Ren asked.

She looked around the room again. The empty space. The open window. The air moving freely.

Yeah, she replied. *I think it is.*

That night, she dreamed of the rooftop. Not the fear. Not the rain. Just the sky, she and Ren.

On the fourth day, she finally picked up a pencil.

Her hand hovered over the blank page, trembling slightly—not from fear, but from uncertainty.

She had never drawn without pain guiding her before. Every line she'd ever made had come from something heavy. Every line she had ever drawn had been the depiction of her pain and survival.

"What do I draw," she whispered, "when I'm not

drowning?"

The pencil touched the paper and they started

communicating. A single line. Then another.

Slowly, deliberately, she drew a cityscape—not overwhelming, not crowded. Just buildings standing side by side beneath a wide sky. In one window, a small light glowed.

It wasn't dramatic.
But it was honest.
When she finished, she leaned back and studied it. Her chest felt tight—but not suffocating.
"I can breathe," she realized. "Even here. Especially here."
For the first time, Tokyo didn't feel like an escape.
It felt like the beginning of something she hadn't yet learned how to name.

CHAPTER TWELVE

Noir Star Is Born

Airi didn't choose the name right away.

For days, she created without labels—drawing quietly at the small desk by her window, sometimes on the floor, sometimes sitting cross-legged against the wall when her thoughts felt too heavy to sit upright. Tokyo moved outside her room in constant motion, but inside, time stretched and softened.

She posted nothing.

Not because she doubted her art—but because sharing meant being seen, and being seen had once nearly broken her. Now she has a different kind of hesitation.

Still, the urge lingered.
Not the urge to be praised. The urge to reach.

One evening, after the sky darkened into a deep, inky blue, Airi opened her laptop. The glow of the screen felt intrusive at first, like an eye opening in the darkness.
She created a new account.

No photo.
No real name.
No explanation.
She stared at the username field for a long time. “I don’t want them to see me,” she thought.
“I want them to see what I leave behind.”

Her gaze drifted to the sketchbook on the desk. The drawings inside it were quieter than before—less crowded with pain, more honest in their stillness. Shadows still existed, but they no longer swallowed the light. Her drawings showed her healing slowly whispering we are proud of you gently.
She typed:
Noir Star

Black, like night.
Star, like something that existed even when unseen.
She uploaded her first piece without a caption.

Just the image.

A lone figure sitting on a rooftop beneath a vast sky. The city below was blurred, indistinct, while the stars above were sharp and deliberate, as if they had been placed there with intention.
She closed the laptop immediately after.
Her heart raced anyway.
“Why does this feel scarier than the bridge?” she wondered, hugging her knees to her chest.

Because this meant staying. This meant surviving the past

and facing it. The response didn’t come all at once.

At first, there was nothing. Hours passed. Then a single

notification appeared. Someone liked your post.

Airi stared at the screen. Then another.

A comment followed.
This feels quiet in a way I didn't know I needed.
Her throat tightened.
She refreshed the page again and again, each time expecting the warmth to disappear—but it didn't. More people found the image. More reactions appeared, soft and thoughtful rather than loud.

It feels like breathing.
I don't know why, but this made me feel less alone.
Thank you for drawing this.
This is showing survival in a very beautiful yet heartbreaking way.
Airi closed the laptop and pressed her forehead against the cool surface of the desk.
Her hands trembled.
"They don't know me," she whispered. "But they understand."

Maybe sometimes getting lost in the journey is important to find yourself.

Days turned into weeks.

She posted slowly, carefully—never forcing herself, never rushing. Each drawing carried a piece of her truth, but not all of it. She learned how to choose what to share and what to keep.

Her following grew quietly.
No viral explosion.
No sudden fame.
Just a steady accumulation of people who stayed.

Just genuine people who connected with her through her art.

One night, as rain tapped gently against her window, a message appeared in her inbox.

Your work is remarkable. I am truly mesmerized by your work. I represent a small independent gallery in Tokyo. We're hosting an exhibition focused on emerging anonymous artists. Would you consider participating?

Airi's breath caught.

She read the message thrice, her heart pounding louder with each word. An exhibition meant space.
Walls.
People standing in front of her work.

It meant being seen without being hidden behind a screen.

She didn't reply immediately.

Instead, she opened her sketchbook and turned to a blank page.

"What am I afraid of now?" she asked herself while filling the paper with her emotions.
The answer came slowly.

That they'll see me clearly—and decide I wasn't worth the looking. Suddenly her phone buzzed.

A message from Ren.
How's Tokyo tonight?
She smiled faintly.
Still loud, she typed.
But I'm learning how to exist in it. Loudness seems peaceful here.

She hesitated, then added:
Something happened today.
Good or bad? he asked.
She looked at the gallery message again.

I don't know yet, she replied. *But it feels...*

important.

Ren responded after a moment.

Then whatever it is—you don't have to face

it alone.

Airi closed her eyes.

For the first time, the name Noir Star didn't feel like a mask. It felt like a beginning that's worth her struggles.

CHAPTER THIRTEEN

Anonymous Light

The cafe was narrow, tucked between two older buildings that looked like they had learned how to endure without complaint. Its sign was small and unassuming, the kind of place most people passed without noticing unless they were looking for quiet. It hurts and heals at the same time, left unseen hurts but being seen also has a constant fear of judgements.

Airi liked it immediately.

She sat near the window, hands wrapped around a warm cup she hadn't yet tasted, watching steam curl upward in delicate spirals. Outside, Tokyo moved in fragments—heels clicking against pavement, umbrellas tilting against the wind, faces passing by in brief flashes.
Here, no one stared.
No one bothered about her.
Her phone lay face-down on the table.
The gallery message had been sitting unread for three days now, not because she hadn't seen it, but because she wasn't ready to answer.

Confused of what she herself wants.
"Airi Takahashi," she thought. "Noir Star."
"Anonymous artist."

Each identity felt separate. Each felt incomplete.
The bell above the café door chimed softly.
A woman stepped inside, pausing briefly as her eyes scanned the room.
She wore a dark coat and carried herself with an easy confidence, the kind that came from knowing exactly who you were.

She noticed Airi immediately.

"You must be Noir Star," the woman said, smiling as she approached. "Or at least, the person behind it."
Airi's breath caught.
"I—" She stopped herself. "I didn't confirm anything."
The woman laughed lightly. "No, but you came anyway."
She extended her hand. "Haru Mori. I curate exhibitions for small independent galleries. Thank you for meeting me."

Airi shook her hand, her grip tentative.

"I wasn't sure," Airi admitted as they sat. "About... all of this."

Haru nodded, unfazed. "That's usually how I know someone is worth talking to."
They spoke slowly at first. About art. About anonymity. About why some people chose to hide their names and others didn't.
"You paint silence," Haru said after a while. "Not emptiness. Silence. There's a difference.... in a beautiful way."
Airi stared into her cup. "Silence can

still hurt."

"Yes," Haru agreed. "But it can also protect."

Haru explained the exhibition—**Light in Shadows**.

A small space. Carefully curated. Artists who had something to say but weren't ready to be exposed entirely. The place where you can leave your impact on others without telling them who you actually are.

"You don't have to reveal anything you're not ready to," Haru said gently. "Your work can speak for you."

The words loosened something in Airi's chest.

"What if people ask who I am?" Airi asked.

"Then you decide how much of yourself you give," Haru replied. "Art doesn't demand confession. Only honesty, which your art already has."

That night, back in her apartment, Airi replied to the gallery message.

I'd like to participate, she wrote.

As Noir Star.

Her hands trembled as she pressed send.

***

The exhibition preparations moved quietly but steadily.

Haru checked in often, offering guidance without pressure.

Airi spent long hours selecting pieces—choosing which parts of herself she was ready to let the world see.

Some drawings were too raw.

Some too fragile.

Some still belonged only to her.

She chose the ones that felt like survival rather than suffering. Ren followed the process from afar.

You sound different lately, he texted one evening. Calmer. Peaceful.
Airi smiled faintly.

I think I'm learning how to stand without shrinking, she replied. I wish I could see it; he wrote.

You will, she thought. Eventually.

On the night she finalized her submissions, Airi stood beneath her window, staring at the stars barely visible through the city's glow.
"I'm still anonymous," she whispered. "But I'm not invisible anymore."

The light didn't come from the spotlight.
It came from choosing to stay.

CHAPTER FOURTEEN

Light in Shadows

The gallery was quieter than Airi expected. When she first stepped inside, she paused just past the doorway, her fingers tightening around the strap of her bag.

The space was small but deliberate— white walls softened by warm lighting, the air carrying the faint scent of fresh paint and wood. Nothing echoed. Nothing overwhelmed. It felt intentional.

Haru noticed her immediately.

"You came early," she said, smiling as she crossed

the room. "I wanted to see it empty," Airi replied.

"Before... people."

Haru nodded, understanding without explanation. "That's usually the hardest version of a place to stand in."

Airi walked slowly along the walls. Her work hung among others—

photographs, abstract canvases, mixed media pieces—but somehow it didn't feel lost. Her drawings didn't shout. They didn't need to.

They waited.

One piece showed a girl seated beneath a night sky, knees drawn close, light spilling faintly from her chest. Another depicted hand reaching toward stars that hovered just beyond touch—not distant, but careful.

Airi stopped in front of the last piece she had almost decided not to include.

It was simple. A figure standing in the middle of an open space, shadows behind her, light ahead. No audience. No applause.

Just choice.

"You almost didn't send this one," Haru said quietly from

beside her. Airi nodded. "It felt... too close."

"That's usually how you know it belongs," Haru replied.

As the opening hour approached, Airi's chest tightened in ways she hadn't expected. Her thoughts circled, restless.
What if they misunderstand?
What if they don't feel anything at all?
What if being unseen was safer?

She moved to a corner of the room, watching as the first visitors entered. Their footsteps were cautious, respectful. Voices stayed low.
People stopped.
They leaned closer.

They stayed longer than she thought they would.

Airi watched a woman stand in front of her work for several minutes, hands clasped tightly together. A man beside her wiped his eyes quickly, as if embarrassed by the gesture.

No one asked who the artist was. They didn't need to.

Airi's phone buzzed.

A message from Ren.

Is it happening now?

She typed back with shaking fingers.

Yes.

How does it feel?

She looked around the room again. At strangers standing quietly with her truth.

Like I'm standing in light without burning, she wrote.

Ren replied almost instantly. *I'm proud of you. You are awesome Airi.*

The words settled into her chest, warm and steady.

As the evening continued, more people arrived. The room filled, but it never felt crowded.

Conversations bloomed softly—about pain, about hope, about how quiet things could still be loud. About how sometimes the silence speaks for you instead of words.

Airi stayed in the background, unnoticed by choice. And for the first time, anonymity didn't feel like hiding. It felt like freedom.

Hiding doesn't always mean running away, sometimes it means choosing peace for your own sake.

CHAPTER FIFTEEN

The Exhibition of Shadows

By the second evening, the gallery felt different. Not louder—just heavier.

Word had begun to spread, quietly at first. The kind of attention that didn't arrive in crowds but in intention. People came looking for something, though many of them didn't seem to know exactly what it was until they found it standing on a white wall beneath warm light.

Airi noticed the change immediately.

Visitors lingered longer now. They stood closer to the drawings, as if proximity might help them understand something unspoken. Conversations became more personal, less careful.

"I felt like this once," a woman murmured to no one in particular.

Another visitor nodded slowly, eyes still fixed on the artwork. "It feels like someone finally put words to something I never could."

"It's deep but in a painful way."
"I wish I could hug this artist."

Airi stood near the back of the room, hands folded in front of her, breathing carefully.

Each comment landed somewhere inside her—not sharply, not painfully—but with weight.

"They're seeing it," she thought. "Not me. But the truth I left behind." A reporter arrived just before closing.

Haru noticed first, her expression tightening only slightly before smoothing out again. She approached Airi quietly.

"We weren't expecting press this soon," she said. "You don't have to speak to them."
Airi followed her gaze.

The reporter stood near the entrance, notebook in hand, eyes scanning the walls with a kind of focused curiosity. Not predatory. Not careless.

Just attentive.
"What do they want to know?" Airi asked softly.
Haru smiled faintly. "Who Noir Star is."
Airi's chest tightened.

"I don't want to lie," she said.

"You don't have to," Haru replied. "You can let your work answer."

The interview was brief.

The reporter asked about themes. About silence. About the way darkness and light coexisted without cancelling each other out.

“This artist doesn’t seem interested in despair,” the reporter said thoughtfully. “It feels more like... survival.”
Airi swallowed.

“That’s because surviving is an act,” she said before she could stop herself. Haru glanced at her—but didn’t interrupt.

“Staying,” Airi continued, voice steady despite the tremor beneath it. “Choosing to stay even when leaving feels easier.”

The reporter nodded, scribbling something down.

“Will the artist ever reveal themselves?”

they asked.

Airi met their gaze.

“Maybe,” she said. “When it stops being the most important question.”

“What makes your art so special?” they continued.

“It came from the moments when I couldn’t speak,” she continued, “When no one heard me I drew instead. I think everyone carries a little shadow inside them. I just wanted to show that light still exists there too. I think in the times of darkness...... when people are about to give up, all they need is a little light to guide them to come out of the darkness and I want my arts to be that light.”

The article went live two days later.

Anonymous Artist 'Noir Star' Captures Quiet Survival in Tokyo Exhibition.

There was no name. No face.

But there were images.
And there were reactions.

Messages poured into the gallery's inbox. Emails. Comments. People asking to buy prints, to share stories, to say thank you. Airi sat alone in her apartment that night, phone glowing softly in her hands. One message stood out.

Your work kept me here today. I didn't think anything could.
She set the phone down carefully.

Her chest tightened, but this time, it wasn't fear. It was responsibility.
"I stayed," she whispered.
"And now... they're staying too."
Outside her window, the city pulsed quietly, unaware of the shift happening inside one small room.
The stars were barely visible. But she knew they were there.

I used to think light was something that burned.......
But maybe, when you stop running from it, it becomes warm instead.
Maybe my arts were the light I was searching for.

***

The TV glows in the dimly lit room as Airi's parents sit silently watching the news broadcast.

"Tokyo's breakout artist Nior Star revealed her emotional story through her debut exhibition today, moving audience across the city."

The TV screen shows Airi standing beside her painting, smiling nervously under the spotlight.

"She looks a lot different now," her mother admits, "She looks a lot happy. Her eyes are full of hope and she has a different kind of glow now, that I have never seen when she was with us."

"She is grown." Her father said, "Stronger than before. Glooming. Shining as she was meant to be."

Silence followed the room.

"I wonder," her mother with tears in her eyes continued, "If she still hates us or forgiven for what we did to her."

"Maybe," her father quietly said, "We deserve it. Maybe we were never capable of being her parents."

"We lost her once... I don't want to lose her again. I want her with me happy and want to give her all the love that we failed to give her when she was with us. I want to make her feel loved and apologize for the wrongs that we did to her." Her mother regretted.

***

Later Mio in her room, scrolls through Airi's social media profile.

She watches a clip from the exhibition, a shot of Airi speaking to the crowd of reporters.

"Onee-chan," Mio teary, "I didn't understand you back then. You always looked lonely, but I thought you were just quiet."

"I didn't see your pain...... I am sorry. I failed to understand you. Maybe it was all my fault that you felt this way. Maybe I was the problem in your life."

She types a message in the comments under one of the Airi's posts.

"Your art...... feels like home. Thank you,

Nior Star." She doesn't sign her name.

Sometimes in life we blame others while sometimes our own self for the things happening, but in reality, it is no one's fault, not even yours.... Just that things need time to fall in place. So, if today you think something is going wrong, hang on there a little longer everything will be fine for sure.

CHAPTER SIXTEEN

The Name the World Learned Too Fast

The first time Airi saw her art shared outside the gallery's page, her chest went cold.
It wasn't dramatic.
It wasn't cruel.
It was casual.

A repost on a popular account. A caption filled with admiration. Comments stacking rapidly beneath it.

Who is this artist?
Does anyone know Noir Star's real name? This feels too personal to be anonymous.
Airi stared at the screen, her fingers hovering just above it. "This wasn't part of the plan," she thought.
The anonymity that had once felt like shelter now felt thin—fragile, stretched by curiosity and hunger. People didn't mean harm.
They rarely did.

They just wanted more.

At the gallery, Haru noticed the shift immediately.

"We need to talk," she said gently, closing the office door behind them.

Airi sat down slowly. "They're looking for me."

"Yes," Haru admitted. "And they will keep looking."

Airi's stomach twisted. "I didn't lie. I never pretended."

"I know," Haru said softly. "But attention doesn't always respect boundaries." That night, her phone wouldn't stop buzzing.

Messages multiplied faster than she could read them. Some were kind. Some invasive. Some dangerously close to guessing.

Airi turned the phone face-down and pressed her palms into her eyes.

"I chose to be seen," she told herself. "I didn't choose to be exposed."

She thought of her parents.

Mio.

The quiet life she had built piece by piece.

And how easily it could unravel. A name is a doorway.

Once opened, it never closes the same way again. I wanted my art to speak.

I didn't know the world would try to answer back.

***

She didn't sleep that night.

Instead, she opened her sketchbook and drew until her hands ached, until her eyes begged her to stop. Faces without features. Crowds without eyes. Light breaking through cracks that hadn't existed before.

In the morning, Haru called.
"They've identified you," she said quietly.

Airi checked her phone. The news breakout saying, "Breaking News: Nior Star's real name in Airi Takahashi – the survivor of the 2018 suicide attempt."

"The mysterious Nior Star has been revealed to be Airi Takahashi...."
"Once a troubled teen, now a celebrated artist."
"Critics divided: Is her fame built on tragedy?"

Screens flicker – news anchors, online threads, and countless faces talking about her name. Some compassionate, others cruel.
Her hands trembling, holding the phone in her hands. The comments flooded on the social media profile.
"She's the girl from that news?"
"Is this some sympathy act?"
"Still.... She's brave."
"I remember her case.... Poor thing."
Seeing all this she throws her phone aside, sobbing not ready to face all this, "Why now....? Why again....? Why when I finally started living? Why.... Is my past haunting me again? Why me again......"

***

Haru in her studio slams her phone shut, frustration in her eyes. Reporters crowded outside the office door.

"Miss Haru," called her assistant continuing, "more calls are coming in – interviews, statements, even TV shows want her"

"Tell them she is resting." Cutting her assistant in between. "No comments until I speak to her myself."

Haru thinking,

They loved her art...... now they want to dissect her soul. Everyone has their past, why can't they let the other person breath when someone is finally trying to get over it? Why is this world so cruel that they can't even understand the other person's pain and emotions?

***

(About a month later)

Airi in her flat with curtains drawn, food untouched, with silence, laptop open with the new notifications of article after article about her "past."

Then she heard a faint knocking sound at her door. She asked who it was, afraid it might be media.

But it replied with, "Airi... it's me. Ren"

She hesitated a little and the opened the door unsure of whether she should or not.

Ren stands there, rain-soaked completely, holding two cans of coffee. He smilingly said, "Thought you might need someone to drink with."

Airi steps aside, letting him in.
After a moment of silence between them, Airi finally broke it.

"They know.... everything. My name, my past,

even.... that day. It's like I am a headline again.
All those years of trying to heal – gone in a flash."
"I saw," Ren continued, "The internet is loud. But they don't get to defy you."

"That's easy to say," Airi said with a bitter smile, "But they are already judging me – 'The broken girl who paints.' I just wanted to be seen for my art, not my scars."

Ren softly "Your scars are your art, Airi. You are able to draw because of those scars only.
Every color, every brushstroke – it came from what you survived. You didn't rise to be perfect, Airi. You rose to be real. Being real means facing everything with the strength and accept what has happened to you in the past and most importantly tell the world that you are already over it. You are strong Airi, more than you think you are, so just go for it."

"But what if being real hurts people? What if I am just... reminding them of their pain? What if instead of pulling them out of darkness I put them into it?" She asked with the trembling voice.

Ren with a soft, gentle tone replied, "Then maybe that's your light. You remind them that they're not alone in the dark. You remind them that the way your arts helped you survive, they can survive too..."

Then there was another knock at the door and this time it was Haru with a small box of pastries.

"If we are going to face chaos, might as well do it with sugar."

Said Haru. "You're not mad?" Airi asked with a faint smile.

"At you?" Haru asked, "Never. At the world? Constantly. Listen – this leak wasn't your fault. Fame is messy. But I believe this will pass.... If you let people see your truth before others twist it."

Airi quietly listens with an unsure look on her face.

Haru continued, "You have already told your story through your paintings. Now it's time that you tell it with words."
That night after listening to Haru and Ren, she finally decides to drop a video message online.
"Hi!
I guess you all know my name now.
I am Airi Takahashi – the girl who once wanted to disappear. but I didn't.
I stayed.
and I painted.
Every canvas I made was a conversation I couldn't have out loud.
I am not perfect. I still have scars. But those scars.... helped me create something honest. Whoever I am today is because of the pain I went through. If scrape out the pain from my life then I won't be who I am today and maybe my art won't talk to you as it does now.
If my story makes you see pain, I hope it also helps you see survival. Both can exist together. I hope my story and art give you the inspiration to keep going even if things don't seem fine, even if things seem impossible, I hope you find strength to survive so that you can see the beautiful future waiting for you. Because I believe that the endings are always happy, if it's not

happy then it's not the end.... So, keep going and don't give up. Thank you.... for seeing me."

After this post of hers, her social media account flooded with a lot of comments about how proud and happy people were that she survived.

***

Later that night, Airi and Ren sit under the starry sky. The city glows beneath them, talking.

Ren started.

"Remember when you said stars felt too far

away?" "Yeah. I thought they were

unreachable."

"Maybe.... You just needed to realize you were one of them."

She looks up, stars shimmering in her eyes, said "Maybe I can shine.... Even if I am cracked. Maybe the universe likes broken things a lot that it makes them beautiful."

Ren smiling, "That's how the light gets out."

Being found is not the same as being understood.
But hiding forever is not living either.

If my name is spoken, then I will decide what it means.
Sometimes, being seen is terrifying.

But in the end.... I learned that light doesn't erase the dark. It just reminds us we've survived it. It reminds us of the strength which was hidden inside us.

CHAPTER SEVENTEEN

Speaking With a Shaking Voice

(Things that happened between that one month)

The email arrived at 11:43 p.m.

Airi noticed the time because she had been watching the clock already— waiting for it to change, as if the night itself might offer permission to sleep. Her room was dim except for the desk lamp, its warm circle of light barely touching the walls. The rest of the apartment lay in shadow, quiet enough that she could hear her own breathing.

The subject line stopped her.

In Your Own Words.

She didn't open it right away.

Instead, she closed her sketchbook carefully, aligning the corners as though order might stabilize something inside her chest. Her pencil lay where she had dropped it, graphite smudged faintly across the page—an unfinished line she hadn't known how to complete.

She opened the email.

The language was polite. Thoughtful. Almost gentle.

We would like to offer you a space to speak for yourself—without cameras, without spectacle. A chance to define your work in your own terms.

Airi leaned back in her chair and stared at the ceiling.

"My own terms," she thought.

"When did that become something, I had to negotiate?"

Her name—her real name—had been moving through the world for days now, carried by articles, reposts, conversations she would never hear directly. She felt it in the way strangers looked at her a second too long. In the way silence no longer felt private.

Her phone buzzed softly.

Ren.

You still awake?

She hesitated, then replied.

Yeah.

Something wrong?

Airi stared at the blinking cursor. They want me to talk.

A pause.

Then:

Do you want to?

She swallowed.

That was the question no one else had asked. Haru called the next morning.

"I don't want to push you," she said carefully. "But I need to be honest with you."

Airi sat on the edge of her bed, sunlight pooling at her feet.

"People are already telling your story," Haru continued. "If you don't speak, silence will speak for you."

Airi closed her eyes.

She had lived inside other people's assumptions her entire life. Quiet meant fine. Withdrawal meant strength. Survival meant she didn't need help.

"I don't want to explain myself again," Airi said softly. "I don't want to turn my life into context."

"Then don't," Haru replied. "Set boundaries. Choose the shape of your voice."

That night, Airi sat on the floor, her back against the wall, knees pulled close. The city outside her window glowed faintly, blurred by distance and glass. She felt suspended—between the person she had been and the one she was becoming, unsure where the ground was.
She opened her laptop again. Read the email slowly.
And wrote back.

I'll speak once.
Written interview only.
No speculation about my personal life.
I will talk about art, silence, and survival.

Nothing else. Her hands trembled when she

pressed send.

The interview was published three

days later. Airi read it alone.

Not quickly. Not bravely.

She read it the way one reads something fragile—carefully,

prepared to stop if it hurts too much.

The questions were restrained. The answers unmistakably hers.

She spoke of art as a place where words failed. Of silence as something that could both protect and suffocate. Of survival not as a victory, but as repetition—waking up, choosing to stay, again and again.

Then she reached the sentence she barely remembered writing.

I'm not here because I overcame anything. I'm here because I stayed.

Her breath caught.

The words looked exposed on the screen, unguarded and honest in a way that made her chest ache. She closed the laptop and pressed her palm flat against her sternum, grounding herself in the steady proof that she was still here.

The response came fast.

Messages poured in—gratitude, recognition, relief. People thanking her for saying what they hadn't known how to say themselves.

And then the other messages.

Accusations. Demands.

Frustration. She's being vague.
She owes us more.
If she wants to help people, she should be

honest. Airi turned her phone face-down.

"I didn't do this to be consumed," she whispered to the empty room.

She opened her sketchbook and drew until her fingers ached—

not finished pieces, not symbols meant to be understood. Just lines. Pressure. Movement.

A figure emerged slowly.

Standing. Not fearless. But present.

I thought my voice would break if I used it.
Instead, it shook—and kept going.

Maybe courage isn't being steady.
Maybe it's speaking anyway.

CHAPTER EIGHTEEN

The Weight of Being Chosen

Mio arrived on a day that couldn't decide what it wanted to be.

The sky hung low and pale, clouds pressing together without rain, as if even the weather was holding something back. Airi stood near the station exit, fingers curled around the strap of her bag, watching people pass in unbroken streams.

She hadn't told herself she was waiting. She had simply came early.

When Mio appeared at the far end of the platform, Airi felt it immediately—a small, sharp recognition in her chest. Her sister looked thinner than she remembered, shoulders drawn in, posture tense in the way of someone who had practiced being careful for a long time.

Mio hesitated before stepping closer. "Onee-chan," she said.

The word sounded heavier than it should have.

Airi lifted her hand in a small wave. It felt safer than an embrace.

They walked side by side toward the exit, their steps unconsciously matching pace but not direction. The space between them wasn't accidental. It was years wide, filled with things neither of them had known how to name.

At the apartment, Mio removed her shoes slowly, aligning them carefully by the door. She sat on the edge of the couch, hands folded in her lap, eyes fixed on nothing in particular.

"I didn't know how to come," Mio said finally. "I kept rewriting what I'd say. None of it sounded right."

Airi poured tea, letting the kettle's soft sound ground her. "You came," she replied. "That counts."

Mio swallowed. "Mom asked me to check on you." Airi nodded once.

"Because people are talking," Mio added quickly. "She was worried."

There it was again—that slight delay before naming who the worry belonged to.

"Were you worried?" Airi asked gently.

Mio's breath hitched.

"Yes," she said immediately. "I just didn't know if I was allowed to be." Airi sat across from her.

The silence stretched—not uncomfortable, but fragile. Like glass about to break but not yet broken.

"I used to think you were unbreakable," Mio said suddenly. "You never cried. You never complained. Whenever I was scared, you were just... there."

Airi looked down at her cup.

"I learned early that being quiet made things easier," she said. "For everyone, at least for others."

Mio's hands clenched. "They watched me so closely. Every cough, every bad dream. I thought that meant you were okay."

Airi's voice stayed steady, but something inside

her shifted. "It meant I was invisible," she said.

"And I got good at it." Tears slid down Mio's face

without warning.

"I didn't want to be chosen," Mio whispered. "I didn't ask to be the fragile one. I just... was."

"I know," Airi replied softly. "That's the cruel part. None of us chose our roles. None of us decided how we were going to be treated."

Mio looked up, eyes red. "I'm sorry," she said. "Not for being cared for. But for not noticing the cost."

The apology didn't erase the past.

But it didn't deflect it either.

That evening, after Mio left, Airi stood by the window and watched the city begin to glow. Lights bloomed one by one, steady and indifferent.

She felt heavy.

But not alone in it.

Some people are protected.
Some people learn to disappear.

Neither is a choice.

Understanding doesn't heal everything.
But it keeps the truth from rotting in silence.

CHAPTER NINETEEN

The Family I Lost

Her mother chose a café halfway between memory and convenience.

Airi arrived early and took the seat by the window, where she could see people before they saw her. The glass reflected her faintly—older than she felt, calmer than she had been allowed to be.

When her mother entered, she didn't look around immediately. She stood just inside the doorway, adjusting her scarf, scanning the room as if preparing herself for impact.

Then their eyes met.

Her mother smiled too quickly.

"Airi," she said, already moving closer. "You look... you

look tired." It was the first thing she noticed. Not

relief. Not worry. Fatigue.

They sat.

The table between them felt narrow and enormous at the same time.

"I've been so worried," her mother began, hands folded tightly around her cup. "Ever since your name started appearing everywhere. People calling. Asking questions."

Airi waited.

"I didn't know what to say," her mother continued. "I kept thinking—how did we miss this?"

The words sounded like regret. They weren't accountability.

"You didn't miss it," Airi said quietly. "You just weren't looking."

Her mother's eyes filled immediately. "We thought you were fine alone," she said. "You were always so calm. So capable. Mio needed us more."

Airi felt the old reflex rise—the instinct to soften, to reassure, to make the room easier for someone else.

She didn't follow it.

"I needed you," she said evenly. "I just didn't know how to compete with being fragile. I just didn't know how to ask for it."

Her mother covered her mouth, tears spilling

freely now. "I'm sorry," she said. "I really am."

Airi nodded once.

"I believe you," she replied. And then, after a pause: "But belief doesn't change what happened."

They parted with an embrace that felt careful, almost ceremonial—like a gesture practiced too late.

Her father arrived two days later.

He chose a different place. Quieter. More practical.

He didn't hug her. He nodded, as if greeting a colleague.

"I read the interview also saw your video confession," he said once they sat. "You were articulate."

Airi almost smiled at the word.

"You always were," he added. "Strong."

The familiar label pressed down on her chest.

"I wasn't strong," she said. "I was silent. And you confused it with strength." He

frowned slightly. "We had responsibilities. We assumed if something was wrong, you'd tell us."

Airi looked at him for a long moment.

"I did," she said softly. "Just not out

loud." He shifted, uncomfortable.

"You never asked," she continued. "And after a while, I stopped believing anyone would."

Her father's jaw tightened. "We did our best," he said.

"I know," Airi replied. "And that's what hurts."

The truth settled between them—not explosive, not dramatic. Just

immovable. When they stood to leave, he hesitated.

"If you ever want to talk," he

said. Airi met his eyes.

"I'm talking now," she replied. "I just needed you to

listen." They parted without anger.

Without reconciliation.

Without illusion.

That night, Airi walked home alone.

The city felt vast, uncaring, steady. She welcomed that. Some things didn't need to change to be livable.

Inside her apartment, she leaned against the door and closed her eyes. She felt grief—not sharp, not overwhelming.

Grief shaped like absence. Not for what she lost. But for what never existed.

And for the first time, she let herself stop searching for it.

Some families don't break. They simply never hold you.

I can mourn what I didn't have without chasing it anymore. Staying doesn't mean waiting.

CHAPTER TWENTY

Falling Stars

The attention didn't arrive like a

wave. It arrived like weather.

Subtle at first. A pressure change. A sense that the air had shifted even when nothing obvious had moved.

Airi noticed it in her body before she noticed it anywhere else.

Her shoulders stayed tense longer. Her breath shortened without warning. She found herself scanning rooms automatically, counting exits, memorizing faces without meaning to. The city—once a place where she could dissolve into motion—now felt alert, watchful.

Her phone buzzed more often. She stopped answering.

At first, the messages were kind.

Your words helped
me.
I felt seen.
Thank you for staying.

She read those slowly, carefully, as if they were fragile objects that could crack if handled too quickly.

Then the tone shifted. Speculation replaced gratitude. Curiosity sharpened into

entitlement. Threads appeared dissecting her drawings as though they were evidence of something unfinished. Someone posted an old photograph of her from school—cropped, blurred, annotated. She looks so normal.

Airi stared at the screen until the words stopped

making sense. "What was I supposed to look like?"

she wondered.

"And why does pain need a costume to be believed?"

She closed the app and placed the phone face-down on the table,

as though it might quiet itself if she refused to see it.

At the gallery, Haru moved carefully around her, intercepting

requests, declining invitations with a politeness that grew firmer by

the day.

"They want interviews," Haru said one afternoon. "Panels.

Features. They want you to talk about mental health."

Airi nodded faintly.

"They don't want my art," she said. "They want my pain to come with

captions." Haru didn't argue.

That night, Airi sat on her bedroom floor with her sketchbook open in front of her. The page was blank. Too white. Too exposed.

She lifted her pencil.
Nothing happened.
Her hand hovered, frozen—not from lack of ideas, but from too many watching eyes she could feel even in an empty room.
"If I draw," she thought, panic blooming, "they'll take it apart."

She shut the sketchbook abruptly and hugged it to her chest, heart pounding.

Ren noticed the silence.

"You haven't drawn," he said gently, standing in the doorway.

"I don't know how to do it safely anymore," she replied.

He came closer but didn't touch her.

"Then don't make anything for the world," he said. "Make something for yourself. Or make nothing. You're allowed to rest."
She looked up at him, eyes tired.

"What if being seen takes away the only thing that kept me here?"

Ren didn't answer immediately.

"Then we find another way," he said finally. "Visibility doesn't get to rewrite who you are."

Later, lying awake, Airi watched the city glow through the window. Neon lights blurred into constellations of their own, artificial and restless.

She thought of stars—how people admired them from a distance, forgetting how violent their lives really were.
"Even stars fall," she whispered. "When too many people stare."

I wanted to be seen.
I didn't know how heavy watching

could be.

If I pull back now,

It isn't failure.
It's survival learning its limits.

CHAPTER TWENTY-ONE

The Space Ren Keeps

Ren never announced that he was staying.
That was the thing Airi noticed most.

There was no declaration, no promise spoken out loud that might later feel like a burden. He simply adjusted his life around the shape of her days, the way someone shifts furniture without commenting on the effort.
When the city felt too loud, he suggested walking routes with fewer people.
When her phone buzzed too often, he placed it face-down beside his own without remark.
When she went quiet, he didn't rush to fill the
space. That kind of presence unsettled her at
first.

She had grown used to attention that demanded performance—concern that required reassurance, care that needed proof. Ren asked for none of it.

One evening, they walked along a narrow street where the shops were closing one by one. Metal shutters rattled down. The smell of oil and rain lingered in the air. Airi kept her hands tucked into her sleeves, shoulders slightly hunched, as if bracing against something invisible.

"I feel like I'm failing," she said suddenly.

Ren slowed, but didn't stop. "At what?"

"At being what they want me to be," she replied. "At being hopeful. Inspiring. Resilient."

He glanced at her then—not sharply, not with

alarm.

"Who asked you to be that?" he said.

She didn't answer.

They walked a little farther.

Later, in her apartment, Airi sat on the floor with her back against the couch. The sketchbook lay open in front of her again, its pages still blank. Ren sat nearby, sorting through loose papers quietly, the sound soft and grounding.

"I'm afraid if I draw again," she said, staring at the page, "it won't belong to me anymore."

Ren considered this.

"Then don't draw what people expect," he said. "Draw what

they can't see."

She laughed softly, humorless. "Like what?"

"Like hesitation," he said. "Like anger that doesn't know where to go. Like rest."

She looked at him.

"No one wants to see that."

"Good," he replied. "Then it stays

yours."

The words stayed with her.

That night, long after Ren had gone to sleep in the other room, Airi remained awake. The city hummed softly beyond the window. She felt suspended again— but this time, there was ground beneath her feet she hadn't noticed before.

She reached for the sketchbook.

Her pencil moved slowly, uncertain at first. She didn't draw figures or stars or anything that could be read as meaning. She drew pressure. Weight. The shape of holding something without dropping it.
When the page filled, she didn't feel relief. But she didn't feel trapped either.
In the early morning, Ren found her still awake.

"You didn't sleep," he said quietly.
"No," she replied. "But I stayed."
He nodded, as if that was enough.

Some people don't save you.
They don't fix the fall.

They make space beside you until standing feels possible again.
Staying doesn't look heroic.
It just keeps happening.

CHAPTER TWENTY-TWO

Being Misunderstood

The misunderstanding did not arrive with cruelty. That was what made it harder to bear.

It arrived wrapped in praise, softened by good intentions, disguised as concern. People spoke gently now, carefully choosing words that sounded supportive while still reaching for something they believed she owed them.

Airi noticed the shift first at the gallery.

A woman stood in front of one of her drawings for a long time—long enough that Airi began to recognize the stillness of expectation.

When the woman finally turned, her expression was earnest, almost relieved.

"I love how honest this is," she said. "Knowing what you went through makes it even more powerful."

Airi felt something tighten behind her ribs. "What do you mean?" she asked quietly.

The woman hesitated, then smiled again, as if the answer were obvious. "Your story. The pain. It's all here, isn't it?"

Airi glanced back at the drawing. It showed a figure standing beneath a fractured sky, light spilling unevenly across the ground. There were no faces. No explanations.

"I didn't put my life on the wall," Airi said. "I put a feeling."

The woman nodded, but her eyes held confusion—disappointment, even. As though something had been withheld.

Later, scrolling through messages she hadn't meant to read, Airi saw the same pattern repeat.

Your work is so brave, knowing what you

survived.

You should talk more about it.
People would understand better if you explained.

Understand what?

That she stayed?
That she lived without a clean
narrative?
That pain didn't arrange itself into
lessons?

One message stopped her completely.

You don't get to be vague when people are depending on

you.

Depending on you.

The weight of it pressed down hard, sudden and breath-stealing.

She closed her phone and sat very still, letting the feeling pass through her instead of away. Her hands shook faintly—not with fear, but with something sharper.

Anger, maybe.

At dinner that evening, Haru watched her carefully.

"They want a version of you they can carry easily," Haru said. "Symbols are lighter than people."

"I don't want to be a symbol," Airi replied. "I want to be allowed to exist without being translated."

Haru nodded. "Then let them misunderstand you."

That sentence echoed long after Airi returned home.

She opened her sketchbook and turned to a fresh page. For a moment, she did nothing. Then she began to draw—not a scene, not a story, but shapes that resisted interpretation. Lines interrupted themselves. Light fractured without resolution.

When she finished, she realized something quietly, almost with surprise. She didn't care if anyone understood this one.

She taped the drawing to the wall anyway—not for an audience, but as proof that not everything needed permission to exist.

Being misunderstood doesn't erase the truth.
It reveals who came looking for answers instead of listening.

I am not a lesson.

I am not a guide.
I am a person who stayed.

CHAPTER TWENTY-THREE

The Choice to Speak

The invitation sat unopened for three days.

Not because Airi didn't know what it was—but because she did.

The envelope lay on the small table near the window, cream-colored and formal, its edges already soft from being moved aside and picked up again. Each time she passed it, she felt the familiar tightening in her chest, the instinctive calculation of cost.

Speaking meant exposure.
Silence meant being spoken about.
Neither felt safe.

On the fourth evening, rain began without warning. It drummed against the glass in uneven rhythms, loud enough to quiet the rest of the city. Airi sat cross- legged on the floor, watching water slide down the window in thin, crooked lines.

She thought about the first time she had learned to stay quiet.

Not a single moment—just a pattern. The way her parents'

attention always moved elsewhere. The way being "fine" earned nods instead of questions. The way silence slowly turned from a habit into armor.

Armor was heavy.

She pressed her palm to the floor, grounding herself in the present. Ren noticed the envelope then.

"You don't have to open it," he said.

"I know," Airi replied. "That's what scares me."

He sat beside her, close enough that their shoulders almost touched, but didn't. "What happens if you don't?" he asked.

She considered the question honestly.

"They'll keep guessing," she said. "They'll decide what I mean for me."

"And if you do?"

"They'll listen," she said slowly. "But only if I speak in a way that doesn't perform."

Ren nodded. "Then speak like you draw."

That night, Airi finally opened the envelope.

A symposium. A small audience. A conversation—not an interview. The words were careful, respectful. There was no promise of safety, only space.

She slept poorly.

Next day she wrote the reply of the envelope.

Later, that night, after talking to Ren and Haru, she understood that she doesn't need to handle everything alone and there are people who would help her, hold her whenever she needs. So, she decides to drop an official video on her social media account.

Speaking isn't courage.
It's consent.

I didn't raise my voice.
I didn't soften the truth.
I stood where I was and let that be enough.

CHAPTER TWENTY-FOUR

What Remains Unsaid

(After the video message was released.)

The tiredness came later.

Not immediately after she spoke. It arrived quietly, like fog slipping into a valley long after the storm has passed.

Airi noticed it the next morning.

Her body felt heavier than usual, movements slowed by something deeper than sleep deprivation. Even lifting her arm to reach for the curtains required a brief negotiation with herself.

She stayed in bed longer than she meant to, staring at the ceiling as light shifted gradually across it.

There was no regret.
That surprised her.

She searched for it instinctively—waiting for the familiar self-critique, the doubt that usually followed any moment of visibility.
It didn't come.

Instead, there was a dull ache behind her ribs. Not pain.

Not sadness. Release.

She moved through the morning carefully. Brushed her teeth. Drank water. Sat by the window and watched a woman across the street hang laundry, each movement deliberate, practiced, unremarkable.

Ordinary.

The thought settled into her gently.

This is what comes after being

honest. Not clarity.
Just ordinariness.

Her phone buzzed once on the

table. She didn't reach for it.

Some messages could wait. Some reactions belonged to other people, not to her.

Later that afternoon, Ren came by with groceries.

He handed her a bag of oranges and moved to the kitchen, the quiet familiarity of the gesture grounding her more than words could have.

They cooked together without speaking much. The sound of chopping, water running, oil heating in the pan—it all felt steady, reassuring.

Halfway through, Airi spoke without

looking at him. "I think people expect

something to change now." Ren glanced

over.

"Do you want it to?"

She considered the question seriously.

"No," she said. "I think I just want to keep living the way I already was—just without hiding."

They ate on the floor, backs against the couch. Outside, evening settled in softly, the city easing into itself.

After dinner, Airi opened her sketchbook.

She flipped through older pages slowly. Early drawings—hesitant lines, cramped compositions. Later ones—bolder, but heavy with tension. She could see herself in them now, not as a mystery to decode, but as a record of someone doing their best with what they had.

She stopped at a blank page near

the end. For a long time, she didn't

draw.

She just rested her hand on the paper, feeling its texture, its quiet invitation.

When she finally moved the pencil, the lines came slowly. A figure seated, not standing. Not falling. Just there—feet on the ground, shoulders relaxed, gaze turned outward but unfocused.

When she finished, she didn't

label it. Some things didn't

need names.

That night, lying in bed, Airi thought about all the things she hadn't said.

The anger she still carried.
The grief that didn't resolve
neatly. The questions with
no audience.

She realized, with a calmness that felt new, that silence wasn't always avoidance.

Sometimes it was choice.

And sometimes, what remained unsaid wasn't

unfinished— It was protected.

Not everything needs a conclusion.
Some truths live better without applause.
I spoke once.
Now I get to rest.
The quiet that follows isn't empty.
It's mine.

CHAPTER TWENTY-FIVE

After the Applause

The city did not change for her. Airi noticed that first.
Buses still sighed to a stop at the corner. Vendors still argued gently over prices. Someone laughed too loudly outside a café, unselfconscious and unburdened. The world went on with a steadiness that felt almost generous.

She walked through it without urgency.

Her body still felt tender, as if something inside had been handled carefully but extensively. Muscles ached in places she hadn't used consciously. Even her thoughts moved slower, rounding corners instead of rushing toward conclusions.

She let them.

At the small park near her apartment, she sat on a bench and watched children chase one another across the grass. Their voices rose and fell without meaning attached—pure sound, pure motion.
She wondered when she had last existed like that. Not free of pain, but free of interpretation.

A memory surfaced—herself at eight years old, sketching on the back of a worksheet while waiting for her parents to finish speaking to a doctor. The drawing had been messy, half-formed. She remembered liking it anyway.

"I didn't stop drawing because it hurt," she thought. "I stopped because no one noticed when I did."

The realization didn't sting the way it once would have. It simply settled into place, another piece of truth allowed to exist without defence.

Later, she met Haru at the gallery.

The space was quiet, sunlight spilling across the floor in wide, pale bands. Airi walked slowly from piece to piece, noticing details she had overlooked before— brushstrokes that faltered, edges left deliberately unfinished.

"You don't have to decide anything yet," Haru said, as if reading her thoughts. "No next exhibit. No statements."

Airi nodded.

"I don't feel empty," she said after a moment. "I feel...

unoccupied."

Haru smiled faintly. "That's how space starts."

On the way home, Ren walked beside her without commentary. They stopped at a convenience store and bought drinks neither of them really wanted. They stood outside, sipping quietly, watching the automatic doors open and close for strangers.

"Do you feel different?" he asked

eventually. Airi considered it.

"No," she said. "But I feel closer to myself."

"Should we paint something," Ren asked, "Something like old times?"

"Old times?" Airi continued, "Maybe we both need that."

"By the way, I never asked you about your past. Tell me about you." Airi said.

After considering the question carefully, he said "What do you want to know?" Airi replied with "Anything that you are comfortable to share."

Ren started.

"It was me, about 10 years old. My farther reading the newspaper, mother busy on the call. There was silence except for the clock ticking. I told them that I got the first price in the art class that day. My father without even looking up at me said "focus on your real subjects, Ren. Art won't feed you." And that day something I learned that silence was safer than disappointment.

Later at the apartment, they drew paintings that they both could co-relate with. Then Ren said, "When I first talked to you back in school. I didn't want to fix you. I just didn't want you to disappear like I once wanted to."

Airi looks at him with a soft gaze and gentle eyes asking, "You wanted to disappear too?"

Ren, smiling sadly answered, "Didn't we all at some point? But.... Maybe we all are waiting for someone to see us. And the universe sent us for each other."

That night, they shared laughter, memories and promises of never letting go of each other.

That night, she dreamed without images.

Just sensation—warmth, weight, the feeling of being held upright by something steady. When she woke, she didn't reach for meaning.

She reached for breath.

In the morning, she cleaned her apartment slowly. Opened windows. Folded clothes. Watered the plant she often forgot about. Each small task felt like a quiet agreement with the day.

When she sat down to draw, it wasn't out of urgency.

It was habit returning gently, like a hand offered

without demand. She didn't think about who might

see it.

She thought about how it felt to make a line and let it end where it

wanted. Outside, the city kept moving.

Inside, something in her had learned a new rhythm.

Not louder.
Not braver.
Just steadier.

After being seen,
there is a strange quiet.
Not loneliness.
Not relief.
Just the body remembering how to live without explaining itself.
I am still here.
And today, that is enough.

CHAPTER TWENTY-SIX

Learning the Shape of Days

Recovery did not announce

itself. It hid in repetition.

Airi began to notice patterns—not the oppressive kind she once used to survive, but softer ones. Morning light that always fell across the same corner of the table. The hum of the refrigerator that sounded louder at night. The way her body now asked for rest before it collapsed into it.
She started walking at the same hour every afternoon.
Not for exercise. Not to clear her head. Just to move.

There was a narrow street behind her apartment where an elderly man fed stray cats every day at four. Airi didn't know his name. She only knew the rhythm of it—the rustle of a bag, the low murmurs he spoke to creatures who trusted him without ceremony.

She watched from a distance at first.

Then one day, one of the cats approached

her shoe. She froze.

Slow movements, she reminded herself. Don't rush tenderness.

She crouched, extended her fingers, felt the soft, tentative brush of fur. The contact startled her more than pain ever had. "Is this how it starts?" she wondered.

"Not with meaning—but with permission?"

That evening, she tried cooking something unfamiliar. The recipe failed. The vegetables burned slightly. She ate it anyway, sitting on the kitchen floor, laughing quietly at the absurdity of feeling proud of something so small.

Later, Ren joined her, carrying two cups of tea. "You seem... here," he said.

"I am," she replied. "It's strange."

They sat without touching, but the space between them felt inhabited now— not empty, not tense.

She told him about the cats. About the burnt vegetables. About how the world felt less like something she had to endure and more like something she was slowly re-entering.

"I don't think I'm healed," she said. "But I think I'm... inhabiting

myself again." Ren nodded. "That's harder than healing."

Casually Ren asked, "Do you ever think about going back home? Don't you miss them?"

Airi replied, "Sometimes. But.... It's complicated. I miss them, can spend a bit time with them but don't think I can live with them."

"Family always is." Ren agreed.

That night, Airi dreamed of walking through a long corridor lined with doors. This time, she didn't open any of them.

She just walked.

And that was enough.

Healing isn't dramatic.
It repeats itself quietly.

It asks the body, again and again,
if staying still hurts less than running.
Some days, the answer is yes.

CHAPTER TWENTY-SEVEN

Mio, Without the Mirror

Mio called without warning.

Her name lit up Airi's screen, unfamiliar in its suddenness. Airi let it ring once. Twice.

Then she answered.

"Are you busy?" Mio asked quickly, as if already preparing to apologize. "No," Airi said. "I'm home."

There was a pause. A breath. "Can I come over?"

When Mio arrived, she didn't look like someone prepared to speak. She looked like someone who had rehearsed silence instead.

They sat across from each other, tea untouched. "I didn't tell them," Mio said suddenly.

Airi waited.

"I didn't tell them how bad it was," Mio continued. "Not because I didn't believe you—but because I didn't know how to live with what it would mean about me."

The words landed without cruelty. Without defence. Just honesty. "I thought if I acknowledged your pain," Mio said, voice shaking, "I'd have to admit how much space I took."

Airi studied her sister's face—the familiar features, now stripped of the protection of illness and parental attention.

"You didn't take it," Airi said quietly. "They gave it."

"But I kept it," Mio replied. "Even when I didn't need anymore." Silence filled the room again—but this time, it didn't divide them. "I don't know how to make it right," Mio whispered.

Airi considered the question carefully.

"You don't," she said. "You just stop pretending it didn't happen."

Mio cried then—not dramatically, not loudly. Just the slow, unravelling kind that comes when someone finally releases a story they've been carrying alone.

Airi didn't comfort her. She didn't need to. Presence was enough. When Mio left, the apartment felt fuller, not emptier.

Airi stood by the window and watched her sister walk away, shoulders lighter, posture uncertain but honest.

She didn't feel closure. She felt continuity.

This wasn't the first time Mio came over to talk like this, but now it can be the last time she came to discuss the past.

Forgiveness isn't forgetting.
It's choosing not to disappear anymore.
We don't return to who we were.
We meet each other where we finally stand.

CHAPTER TWENTY-EIGHT

Art Without Witness

Airi stopped sharing her work. Not as a statement. Not as resistance. She simply... didn't.

She filled sketchbook after sketchbook with drawings no one else would see. Abstract forms. Half-finished figures. Pages where the pencil barely touched the paper.

One afternoon, Haru found her sitting on the gallery floor, surrounded by pages. "These aren't for exhibition, are they?" Haru asked.

"No," Airi replied. "They're for survival."

Haru smiled. "Good."

That night, Airi taped a single drawing to her bedroom wall. It wasn't beautiful. It wasn't symbolic.

It was honest.

A figure seated on the ground, knees drawn in—not collapsing, not rising. Just staying.

She stood back and looked at it for a long time.

"I used to think art was how I explained myself," she thought. "But maybe it's how I listen."

She slept deeply that

night. No dreams.

Just rest.

Art doesn't owe the world clarity.
Sometimes it only owes the maker
breath.

I am not hiding.
I am choosing where to exist.

CHAPTER TWENTY-NINE

When the Future Stops Demanding Answers

The future used to arrive like an interrogation.

Every question sharpened. Every choice weighed against outcomes she couldn't see but felt responsible for. Airi had lived for years as if tomorrow were a test she might fail without warning.

Now, the days came softer. Not kinder—just quieter.

She noticed it one morning while standing in line at the bakery. The woman ahead of her debated between two kinds of bread with exaggerated seriousness, as if the decision carried moral weight. Airi watched, amused, aware of how unimportant—and how precious—the moment was.

When it was her turn, she chose without thinking. The ease surprised her.

She took the bread to the small park nearby and ate slowly, crumbs falling onto the bench. A sparrow hopped close, fearless. Airi broke off a piece and held it out.

The bird hesitated, then accepted.

She felt something warm spread through her chest—not joy, not relief.

Trust.

Later that day, Ren asked a question he had been

holding back. "Do you think about what comes

next?" he asked.

They were walking along the river, water moving steadily beside them, unconcerned with direction.

Airi considered the question.

"I think about what I want to protect," she said finally. "Not what I want to become."

Ren nodded. "That sounds... sustainable."

That night, Airi lay awake thinking—not about goals, but about textures. The feel of paper under her palm. The weight of tea in a cup. The sound of someone breathing in the next room.

She realized she wasn't afraid of the future

anymore. She just wasn't trying to solve it.

The future used to ask me to explain myself.
Now it waits.
I don't owe it certainty.
Only presence.

CHAPTER THIRTY

The House That Holds Quiet

Airi returned to her childhood home alone. She hadn't planned to. The train ride felt longer than she remembered, the stations unfamiliar despite their names. When she stepped off at the platform, the air smelled faintly of dust and old rain.

The house stood exactly where it always had. Smaller than memory. Quieter.

Her parents weren't home. She hadn't told them she was coming. The key still fit.

Inside, the rooms felt preserved rather than lived in. Furniture untouched. Photos arranged carefully on shelves—Mio at different ages, smiling, celebrated.

Airi walked slowly.

Her old room was at the end of the hall. She opened the door and stopped.

The space was almost empty now. A bed. A desk. No drawings on the walls. No evidence that she had ever stayed long enough to leave a trace.

She sat on the floor.

Not to grieve—but to witness.

"This is where I learned to be small," she
thought. "And this is where I survived
anyway."
In the kitchen, she found an old notebook shoved into a drawer. Her handwriting stared back at her—messy, urgent, alive.
Sketches of stars. Of hands reaching. Of figures half-erased. She closed the notebook gently.

"I don't need to take you with me," she said aloud. "You already did your work." When she left the house, she locked the door carefully.

Not out of duty.
Out of respect.

I don't have to reclaim the past.
I only have to stop carrying it.
Some rooms taught me silence.
Others taught me endurance.
Neither gets to decide who I am now.

CHAPTER THIRTY-ONE

A Small, Unnamed Joy

Joy didn't arrive with fireworks. It slipped in quietly, uninvited.
Airi noticed it while washing dishes one evening. The water was warm. The window open. Music played softly from Ren's phone in the other room.

She caught herself humming. The sound startled her.

She turned off the tap and listened—waiting for the feeling to disappear, the way happiness often had in the past.

It didn't.

Later, Ren joined her on the couch, legs barely touching. "You seem lighter," he said.

"I think I forgot joy doesn't have to announce itself," she replied.

She picked up her sketchbook and drew without thinking.

No intention.

No meaning.

Just motion.

When she looked down, she saw a simple image: two figures sitting side by side, not touching, but close enough that their shadows overlapped.

She smiled.
Not because it was profound. But because it was true.
Suddenly her phone started ringing.
It was Haru calling her.

"Airi there is an exhibition happening and your paintings will be the center of that. What do you think should I say?"
Airi still confused and shocked.

"You don't need to answer immediately. Think about it carefully and answer when you feel like. But it's a big opportunity to lose."

Joy isn't the opposite of pain.
It's what survives beside it.

I don't chase happiness.
I notice when it stays.

CHAPTER THIRTY-TWO

When the Stars Stop Watching

Airi stopped thinking about the stars for a while. That surprised her, when she noticed. They had once been everything—symbols, witnesses, silent observers she projected her endurance onto. She had searched the sky for proof that something distant could still see her when no one nearby did.

Now, weeks passed without her looking up.

It wasn't indifference.

It was relief.

One evening, Ren pointed it out without accusation. "You haven't drawn the sky in a while," he said.

Airi paused, pencil hovering above the page.

"I don't need it to look back at me anymore," she said after a moment.

They were sitting in the balcony, the city spread beneath them like a living map. Windows glowed softly. Somewhere below, a train rattled past, steady and unconcerned.

Ren leaned against the railing. "Do you miss it?"

She considered the question carefully.

“No,” she said. “I think I mistook being watched for being held.”

That night, she dreamed of standing beneath a blank sky—not dark, not lit. Just space. And instead of feeling lost, she felt grounded, aware of her own weight, her own warmth.

She woke calm.

The next morning, Haru called again, “Asking for her answer.”

She was still confused but answered, “I am ready for this but after this I'll not be doing any further exhibitions.”

Haru agreed happily.

I once needed the stars to remember me.
Now I remember myself.

Being seen is not the same as being safe.
And safety doesn't require an audience.

The Day Nothing Happens

The day nothing happened became important later. At the time, it felt unremarkable.

Airi woke up without dread. She made coffee that tasted slightly bitter. She spilled a little water on the counter and wiped it up without annoyance.

No revelations arrived.

No memories ambushed her.
No messages demanded response.

She went out for groceries and forgot one thing she meant to buy. She shrugged and kept walking.

In the afternoon, she sat at the table and drew for hours. Not intensely. Not urgently. Just steadily, as if the act itself had finally detached from purpose.

When Ren came home, he found her surrounded

by pages. "You worked a lot," he said.

"I rested," she replied.

They ordered food and ate on the floor. Outside, rain began softly, not dramatic enough to be called a storm.

As night settled in, Airi felt a strange gratitude—not for happiness, not for healing, but for neutrality.
"I used to think nothing happening meant I was disappearing," she thought. "But this is what staying looks like."

Peace doesn't announce itself.
It blends in.

If no one is watching, and nothing demands proof—
I am still here.

CHAPTER THIRTY-THREE

Light Beyond Pain

Sunlight pours through wide windows. The room is alive – canvases, paints, soft chatter.

The sign near the entrance reads:
"STARLIGHT FOUNDATION - ART FOR HEALING"
Airi stands at the doorway, watching young artists set up nervously.

Pain doesn't disappear.
But it can be shared, shaped.... Understood.

Inside the foundation, a teenager hesitates before a blank canvas. "What if it looks wrong?"
Airi kneeling beside them, "Then it's honest. That's enough to begin."

Mio Learns to Stand Alone

Airi noticed the change in Mio slowly.

It wasn't something her sister announced. It showed up in small shifts—shorter messages, firmer boundaries, decisions made without seeking reassurance.

They met for lunch on a weekday, the restaurant nearly empty.

Mio talked about work. About a move she was considering. About things that didn't orbit illness or apology.

At one point, she stopped mid-sentence.

"I don't need you to take care of me anymore," Mio said quietly. "I just wanted you to know."

Airi felt something loosen inside her.

"I know," she said. "I stopped a long time ago."

Mio smiled—not sheepishly, not guiltily. Just honestly.

***

Mio enters the foundation carrying boxes of supplies. "I didn't know paint brushes came in these many sizes."

Airi laughs softly, "Neither did I – until I needed all of

them." They arranged the materials together.

"I am glad you let me help." "I am glad you asked."
Young artists painting emotions with bold colors. Mio encouraging a child, handing them fresh paper.
Airi guiding hands gently, never correcting – only supporting.
A wall slowly filling with the artwork titled "What I Feel."
Beauty doesn't come from pretending pain never existed.

It comes from choosing to speak anyway. It comes from admitting

what hurts.
After leaving the foundation they both went to Airi's apartment. They sat beside each other.

"Do you ever wish things were different?" Mio asked.

Airi thinks.
"Sometimes. But then..... I see this place. And I know why I stayed. If things were different then I could have never came here."

Pain may shape us.....
but love teaches us where to grow.
Light doesn't erase the past,
It shows us the way forward.

The Last Painting

The studio was silent or maybe she felt it that way because she went there after a long time.

Sunlight spills across an enormous blank canvas – larger than any Airi has worked on.
Airi stands before it, paint-strained apron on, hair loosely tied.
She breathes in.
Not nervous.
Ready.

Not an ending,
Just a place to restart.
Haru watches from a distance.

"People are already asking what is next."

"For the first time, I don't know.
And I am okay with it."

Haru smiles as Airi continues to paint.

Bold strokes of warm light.
A path forming from shadow into brightness.
A girl walking forward – not running, not escaping. Figures appearing around her:

Ren, Mio, Children from foundation,
Shapes suggesting her parents – not perfect, but present.
Home isn't a place you return to.
It's a place that finally opens.
Ren enters quietly, carrying tea. He stops, stunned by the canvas. "It feels.... Warm."
Airi nods.
"It's the first time I didn't paint pain first."
"What will you call it?"
Airi looking at the painting, "Home."

Painting the final brushstroke, she steps back.
The painting glows – not literally, but emotionally. A girl walking into light,
surrounded,
unafraid.

She says, "I am not lost anymore."

The Exhibition's center was the painting called **Home – by Airi**
For those still searching.
She thought, "I once asked the world to love me. Now..... I love living."

Closure is not forgetting.
It is arriving.

CHAPTER THIRTY-FOUR

The Reunion

(After the final exhibition, Airi was invited to the award show.)

A familiar hall, but the atmosphere feels different tonight – warmer, quieter.

Airi stands backstage, adjusting the microphone clipped to her dress. Her hands are steady.
I once stood on stages wishing I could disappear. Now I stand here..... choosing to stay.
Her eyes slowly moved across the seated audience – artists, advocates, young students.
Then it stops.
Airi's parents sit together in the front row.
Not stiff.
Not distant.
Nervous.... And proud.

Airi's breath catches – not in fear, but surprise.

Airi steps on the stage as her name is announced. Applause filled the hall. She bows lightly, then looks up – and meets her parents' eyes.

Her mother pressed a hand to her mouth. Her father nods, eyes shining.

Airi starts talking.

"For years..... I searched for love. In approval.... In silence..... In places that didn't know how to give it."

A soft ripple moves through the audience.

"I thought being strong meant never needing help. I was wrong. Being strong is knowing when and how to ask for help when your world is crumbling and you can't fix it anymore." She continues speaking while placing one hand over her heart. "Now, I give love – To those who once felt invisible. To those who were quite not by choice...... but because no one asked them to speak. Because love is something, when you start giving without expecting, finds its way back to you multiplied. To all those listening to me – you matter. Not because of what you achieve..... but because you exist."

Her voice doesn't break.

It steadies.

Applause rises – long, powerful, emotional. Some stand while others wipe their eyes.

Ren smiles softly, pride without possession.

That day she understood, art doesn't save the world, But it reminds us why it's worth saving.

As Airi was about to step down the stage, the host made an announcement, "Tonight, here are people who watched this journey of Nior Star from the very beginning."

Airi turns confused. Her parents stand.

The audience murmurs softly as they walk towards the stage.

Airi's mother reaches her first.
She hesitates a little then opens her arms.
Airi steps forward. They embrace.... Tightly.... Honestly..... for the first time. Tears fall freely.

Her father joins them, placing a hand on Airi's shoulder, voice trembling, "We are.... so proud of you."

After a moment, Airi pulls back slightly, still holding her parents' hands. She takes a breath.
"I carried many questions for a long time." She continued while looking at her parents, "But today.... I choose to carry something else. I forgive you."

Her mother after listening those words breaks down quietly like some heavy burden was removed from her chest and that now she is finally free from the guilt. Her father closes his eyes, relief washing over him.
Ren watching them from a distance, eyes soft, unmoving.
"Forgiveness doesn't rewrite the past.
It releases the future."

Airi standing alone on the stage after her parents left, thinks
Healing doesn't happen alone. Sometime..... it happens when someone finally shows up.
My story isn't special. What's special.... Is how many stories were waiting to be heard.

Later, after the show ended. Airi was removing the microphone when Ren suddenly entered there.
"Airi....." He calls her hesitantly.

"You saw right..... I ..... I finally forgave my parents. It doesn't hurt that much now. Forgiving them seems easier now. I think I'm finally releasing my past." Airi said excitedly, not listening to him properly.

Ren comes close to Airi, distant enough that they won't touch each other but close enough that could feel each other's breath.

"Airi..... I wanna tell you something"

"Yes... go on." She replied sensing the closeness between them.

"I'm not afraid of you leaving," he said. "I'm afraid of asking you to stay before you're ready."

Airi felt the words settle into her carefully.

"I don't feel trapped here," she replied. "That's new."

"Airi, I want to be the person you can rely on for your rest of life. I want to be your comfort zone, Airi" he said. "Will you let me be?"

"No," Airi understanding the depth of the words settling into her heart replied. "Is it something you need to ask me? Isn't it obvious that you are already my comfort zone?"

The love I waited for so long came late.
But it came honest.

Forgiveness isn't forgetting.
It's choosing peace.
It's like finally releasing yourself.

A Letter Never Sent

Airi wrote the letter in one sitting. She didn't plan to. The paper was already on the table, the pen already in her hand. The words arrived without urgency, without careful shaping.

She wrote to her parents.
Not to accuse.
Not to reconcile.
Just to state.

She wrote about the silence. About being "easy." About learning to carry her own fear so no one else would have to.

She didn't soften it.

She didn't sharpen it either.

When she finished, her hand ached—not from effort, but

from honesty. She folded the letter once.

Then again.

She placed it in a drawer and closed it gently.

"I don't need you to read this," she thought. "I needed to write it."
The relief surprised her.

Some truths aren't meant to travel. They just need somewhere safe to land.

CHAPTER THIRTY-FIVE

THE RETURN TO WHERE IT BEGAN

The school bell rings.

Students walk in groups, laughing, chatting – life moving forward. A black car stops outside the gate.

Airi steps out.
She pauses.

The building looks smaller than she remembers.... But the memories feel vast. This is where my voice grew quiet.
And where it finally learned to speak.

As Airi slowly walks into the corridor. Lockers line the walls. Sunlight spill through familiar windows. A bulletin board displays student artwork.
She stops in front of one sketch – raw, emotional.

"Someone's telling the truth here."

A teacher approaches her. "They've been inspired by your story." Airi nods, touched.

She asked about Ms. Nakamura.

Then she got to know that she has left the school long ago and now the school is not in contact with her. She also got an assurance that she must have seen her on the TV and she must really be proud of her.

Airi has been called to her school to inspire young minds.
Airi stands nervously backstage behind the curtain, holding cue cards but doesn't look at them.

Ren stands nearby. "Nervous," he asked.
"A little." She replied. "But this time.... I'm not alone."
Hearing her, Ren smiled.
Airi steps up the stage. The room quiets. Hundreds of students watched her – curious, attentive.

Airi looks at them and then at the empty seat in the back row where she once sat alone.
"I used to sit right there.... Wondering if anyone would notice if I vanished." Airi
started and the room grew still. "I once wanted to disappear. Now I live – so others never have to feel invisible. If you ever feel small or unheard.... Please remember this – Your presence matters more than you know."
Later one of the students handed her a note.
It said, "Thank you for staying."

I didn't disappear.
I became the light.

Your story may begin in silence,
but it doesn't have to end there.

STARDUST MEMORIES

It was a gentle morning with pleasant weather, seagulls gliding in the sky when she received a message from Mio that she is coming over.

Life doesn't need to be loud ...... to be beautiful.

Sunlight fills the home.

Mio and Airi are in the kitchen cooking pancakes when Mio flips it saying, "If these burn, we're calling it modern art."

Airi and Mio starts laughing on it.

"Then I'll frame them." Airi said teasingly.

Ren entered the room right then with coffee mugs.

"Breakfast masterpiece, coming right up."

They ate together at a wooden table, laughter easy and natural.

Then Airi sets up her canvas. She paints slowly – no rush, no pressure. The colors were light this time:

Blues, soft gold, gentle whites.

Ren sits nearby, reading. Mio doing her work.

"Your paintings feel different." Mio said looking at

the canvas.

"So do I." Airi claimed.

Later in the evening that day, all three sit together watching

the horizon.

Ren asked, "Do you ever miss the spotlight?"

“I found something brighter.” She said while shaking her head. “You found home.” Mio said leaning towards her.

I thought I was made of broken pieces.
Turns out... I was a stardust all along.

Some memories hurt.
Some heal.
Some become light.

CHAPTER THIRTY-SIX

When the Stars Remembered Me

Airi returned to the same bridge from where her story of transformation started. The bridge where she was about to give up on everything, but found something precious instead that was worth her life.

The river glimmering in the moonlight like distant memories. The wind moves gently touching her face.
She stands alone at first, hands in her coat pockets. She looks up.

"I used to come here searching for answers..... wondering if I mattered at all."

She remembers young Airi standing alone, clutching sketchbook to her chest, a sky that felt too vast that day.
"I survived something I didn't have words for back then."

As she dived into the memories which were not sharp or painful.

Ren steps beside her and gently wraps his arm around her shoulders. He didn't speak. They just stood together, looking at the sky.
"You didn't come here to escape

anymore." "No, I come here to

remember."

Airi tilts her head upward, eyes reflecting starlight.

"I thought I was forgotten.... But even the stars never stopped

watching." Ren tights his arms slightly – reassuring, present.

The stars upward seems brighter tonight as if they are also happy that she has now finally started living what she was up to and now that she has someone whom she can rely on, they seem to be relaxed.

Slowly – almost imperceptibly – they align.

The constellation forms a girl holding a paintbrush, reaching upward. Not dramatic. Not glowing unnaturally. Just quietly there.

Ren and Airi stood together beneath the sky for a long time. Small. Seen. Enough.

I thought the stars remembered me.
But they were never the ones who had to.

I stayed.
I learned my own name in quiet.
And that was enough.

I am not the girl who want to disappear anymore.
I am the woman who stayed.

If you feel invisible –
Look up.
You are remembered.